ALL ABOUT SPORTS

Sport Climbing

Weight   kilograms × 2.2046 = pounds (lb)
grams × 0.0353 = ounces (oz)

Length   centimeters × 0.3937 = inches   1 cm = $^3/_8$ inch
2 cm = $^3/_4$ inch
3 cm = 1$^1/_4$ inch
4 cm = 1$^1/_2$ inch
5 cm = 2 inch

ft	m	ft	m	ft	m	Temperature	
						°C	°F
1	0.3	30	9.1	800	243.8		
2	0.6	35	10.7	900	274.3	0	32
3	0.9	40	12.2	1000	304.8	5	41
4	1.2	45	13.7	1500	457.2	10	50
5	1.5	50	15.2	2000	609.6	15	59
6	1.8	75	22.9	2500	762.0	20	68
7	2.1	100	30.5	3000	914.4	21	70
8	2.4	200	61.0	3500	1 066.8	22	72
9	2.7	300	91.4	4000	1 219.2	23	73
10	3.0	400	121.9	5000	1 524.0	24	75
15	4.6	500	152.4	10 000	3 048.0	25	77
20	6.1	600	182.9			26	79
25	7.6	700	213.4	*Exact conversion:*		27	81
				1ft = 0.3048m		28	82
						29	84
						30	86

m	ft	m	ft	m	ft
1	3.3	30	98.4	800	2 624.7
2	6.6	35	114.8	900	2 952.8
3	9.8	40	131.2	1000	3 280.8
4	13.1	45	147.6	1500	4 921.3
5	16.4	50	164.0	2000	6 561.7
6	19.7	75	246.1	2500	8 202.1
7	23.0	100	328.1	3000	9 842.5
8	26.2	200	656.2	3500	11 482.5
9	29.5	300	984.3	4000	13 123.4
10	32.8	400	1 312.3	5000	16 404.2
15	49.2	500	1 640.4	10 000	32 808.4
20	65.5	600	1 968.5		
25	82.0	700	2 296.6	*Exact conversion:*	
				1m = 3.2808ft	

ALL ABOUT SPORTS

Sport Climbing

KÖNEMANN

CONTENTS

PREFACE

Sport Climbing is an entirely new sporting manual, for a sport that is in its youth and only just emerging. However, before talking of climbing as a sport, it is necessary to define it, as there are still many uncertainties – especially among those who have no direct experience of it – when it comes to identifying the various attributes that distinguish climbing in general from "freestyle" climbing and "sport climbing" in particular.

When it first began, only a few decades ago, lively arguments also arose, until the inevitable distinction was made between mountain climbing and "free climbing." Today it may be said that sport climbing corresponds to the most natural method of climbing, without the aid of artificial means of advancement. It is carried out, whether at amateur or competition level, on either natural or artificial rock faces, along routes that are totally equipped and controlled from the base.

This makes it a sport that takes place in completely safe conditions, attached by a rope and backed up (or belayed) by a partner (or belayer). Perhaps it seems superfluous to specify this, but it does help to explain, to anyone who still only has a very hazy idea about it, what the possibilities and limitations of this sport are. It is not to be

confused with mountaineering or with traditional freestyle climbing, which involves climbing rock faces without any artificial aids, attaching protection to the rock wall as you advance. Sport climbing is strongly rooted in the traditions of Alpine mountaineering. It is an offshoot of free climbing, but it

has now become completely separate from it, by continuing to evolve on natural rock structures that are sometimes a very long way from mountains, and has managed to overcome difficulties that for a time were beyond the wildest imagination.

Although still relatively young, sport climbing has already developed its own clear identity as a sport among both amateur followers and professionals.
– On an amateur level it is a fantastic sport that can be enjoyed by anyone, given that risk factors are almost non-existent.

climbing; it describes equipment and techniques, from the simplest movements through to detailed descriptions of the movements that make progress more effective, and offers help for overcoming problems on difficult sections. It also deals with fitness training and the world of competition, enabling those who are no longer complete beginners to improve their performance, as well as providing information on how to find the most beautiful cliffs and boulders in the world, where this sport can be practiced at its most challenging level. Above all, this book gives an insight into the essence of this sport, which many take up for fun, only to find that it then becomes a passion, stretching to the utmost limit the athletic abilities of those who practice it. It is a sport that also liberates the mind and spirit in a way that perhaps no other can.

– On a professional level it is controlled by regulations and classifications drawn up by national federations, which in turn are controlled by the ICC (International Climbing Council), and is now carried out almost exclusively on artificial structures. It is also recognized by the CIO (International Olympic Committee).
This book supplies basic information for anyone who wishes to take up sport

1

THE HISTORY

From the pioneers of mountain climbing to the first attempts at sport climbing in Europe and in the United States. The emergence of a new sport.

MOUNTAINEERING, THE ORIGINS OF CLIMBING

Sport climbing, as a sport that can be grasped and practiced by anyone, is a very young sport that has recently become independent from the Alpine mountaineering from which it originates. Mountaineering in its turn developed rapidly from the end of the 18th century as a "conquest" sport. On August 8, 1786 the summit of Mont Blanc was reached for the first time. From then on it was a mad race to conquer other Alpine peaks, a race which sadly claimed the lives of many early climbers, driven on by the desire to be the first to reach still virgin peaks, but aided by nothing but the most primitive equipment, and with no precise knowledge of the risks involved. In 1865, with the first ascent of the Matterhorn, all the most important Alpine peaks had been conquered; the pioneering period was over and the now famous exploration and conquest of mountains all over the world began. During this time, while climbers were first reaching

Below: Mont Blanc, the first summit of the Alps to be conquered in 1786 (photo A.R. Bisson, 1861).
Above: the west face of the Petit Dru remained untouched until 1952 (photo G. Rossat-Mignod).

Himalayan and African peaks, climbing in Europe became increasingly a matter of athletic performance, with climbers seeking ever more direct and challenging routes to reach the peaks. So climbing first appeared within the ambit of mountaineering as a specialized technique for tackling increasingly demanding rock walls.

But as the difficulty increased, so too did the risk of falls, and this led to a new preoccupation with safety. During the 1920s the use of a rope (used only occasionally in the pioneering period) became common practice, together with the first pitons (or bolts) to which the rope could be attached to get over difficult sections.

At about this time the practice of climbing rock walls of moderate height (cliffs) and boulders was introduced, as a preparatory activity for mountaineering. It served both as a way of keeping fit at times when the weather made mountaineering impossible, and as a way of training to overcome the most difficult sections which might subsequently be encountered during a climb.

Left: rope was the first safety measure to be used in climbing (photo E. Frisia).
Above: steel pitons and karabiners first made their appearance in the thirties.
Below: Phillimore and Raynor (seated), two pioneers of mountaineering in the Dolomites in the second half of the 19th century.

the period preceding the Second World War, pure climbing remained almost everywhere as a training exercise, devised as a preparation for real mountaineering.

Exceptions

There were, however, some notable exceptions. In eastern Germany, on the Elbsandstein rocks on the outskirts of Dresden, it became common practice from the start of the 20th century to practice free climbing, using artificial aids only for safety and not as a means of progression. This was an extremely modern concept at the time, but presumably, owing to the existence of the Iron Curtain, it did not spread to the rest of Europe. In this corner of Europe a form of free climbing had developed with its own rules that are still valid today: only rock masses not accessible by any path could be climbed; the routes could be fitted with expanding bolts, fixed at a distance of not less than 13–16 feet (4–5m) apart; and artificial aids such as throwing ropes, being secured from above, or using ladders were forbidden. Lastly, there was an official commission which kept careful note of every successful climb, based on detailed information supplied by the climbers (date of each

Both in climbing schools and on the mountain these climbers used traditional equipment: knee-length corduroy trousers, woolen shirts and heavy shoes. The appearance of the rubber Vibram sole was a great innovation, which led to huge improvements in climbing technique. In

attempt, number of safety points, etc.), with a maximum time allowed to complete a route of three years from the first attempt. This was certainly the first form of free climbing, with extremely modern rules and criteria.

Whereas in Dresden climbing was controlled by strict rules, in the Peak District (England) from the end of the 19th century onwards a tradition had evolved that had been accepted by the mountaineering community. It was based on a deep respect for the rock face itself, which meant only using natural protection (rope slings, stones and bolts driven into the rock), while the use of fixed bolts, considered almost sacrilegious, was strictly forbidden. Even today, on the Peak District gritstone bolts are never used; climbing technique has clearly evolved, but the idea at the root of it has remained the same.

The Yosemite school

In the meantime, in the United States, climbers were marking out the first really demanding routes, from a technical and

Above left: it was in the Dolomites that the "sixth grade" was first made; on rock soft climbing shoes with Vibram soles were preferable to heavy boots. Above: new climbing horizons were opened up in the Yosemite Valley (USA) at the end of the fifties.

sporting point of view, on the granite rock faces of California, but it was not until the end of the 1950s that the immense walls of the Yosemite Valley were successfully tackled. Far removed from, and totally unconditioned by, European mountaineering traditions, these Californian climbers began a new movement in the history of climbing. Their goal was no longer to reach the top, but to achieve the highest technical mastery of the sport, by overcoming the greatest difficulties either out in the wild or in artificial surroundings. It was no longer

a struggle against the Alps, but a quest to find the most eye-catching and demanding route, and a desire to overcome ever stiffer challenges. In a short time two trends emerged, which still exist side by side in America. On the one hand there was a great rise in those who got their thrills from artificial climbing structures, that were increasingly demanding on a technical level, and on the other there was the birth of free climbing, in which the objective was not the climb itself, but "how" it was performed. This meant that they accepted the conditions and problems presented by a rock wall, and attempted to overcome them without using artificial means.

As people's attitudes changed, so did the method of tackling the wall and the type of equipment used: heavy boots were discarded for lightweight climbing shoes with soft soles, and knee-length trousers and checkered shirts exchanged for more comfortable, younger, and lighter materials. This meant that climbers, freed from unnecessary weight, could communicate

Above: the great Yosemite Valley; on the left El Capitan and in the background Half Dome.

more intensely with the natural environment, find pleasure in the movements themselves, progress with nothing but their own strength, in a continuous effort to overcome their own limitations. An essential aid for climbers today is magnesite, used to keep their hands dry. At the end of the 1970s magnesite arrived in Europe, and like every new phase in development, it was keenly defended by the new generation and condemned by the traditionalists. Its opponents saw it as an artificial aid, its supporters simply as an advance in technology, just like climbing shoes. And since magnesite is a very basic prop for climbers, in the end its detractors had to give way, and ever since then the leaders of the climbing world have continued to leave their white prints on the rock.

Free climbing in Europe

The English first introduced this form of climbing in Europe, bringing it from the granite of the Yosemite valley to the still virgin limestone of the Verdon gorges in France. Or to be more precise, it was Fritz Wiessner, a climber from the renowned Dresden school, who first took it across the Atlantic, when he fled to the United States from Nazi Germany. In 1935 he discovered Shawangunks near New York (still the most famous cliff on the East Coast), where he gave free climbing a new start outside Germany; it was actually Wiessner who started off the free climbing movement of the 1960s. So free climbing came to the United States from the Old Continent, and in fact, in the early 20th century, American climbing took place almost entirely on artificial walls. This new concept caught on rapidly in America, but it was to be almost another 40 years before it came back across the Atlantic and gained popularity all over Europe. Actually, free climbing only became common practice here in Europe in the mid-seventies, thus forming the basis of what would become sport climbing.

The early years were not free of controversy, largely because some climbers, perhaps too steeped in the traditions of Alpine mountaineering, interpreted free climbing as an extreme form of climbing done almost without any protection (until it was almost the American free-solo style). The sport ran the risk of turning into a new form of thrill-seeking for the elite, which, owing to the danger involved, could no longer be considered as a sport open to all.

Above: the Verdon gorges, in the south of France, were some of the first adventure grounds for European climbers in the sixties and seventies.

A new sport is born

The first competitions put an end to this tendency. The first international sport climbing contest took place in Bardonecchia in Italy, and was a great success with both participants and spectators. From this date onwards European federations began to form, and it became necessary to produce a stricter definition of the sport, from the point of view of both professionals and enthusiasts, so that it might be easily understood and practiced by anyone, anywhere. The first international competitions in the United States were also organized at about this time, and the first official World Cup took place in 1989. Sport climbing is now practiced all over the world, and is continually evolving. The scale of difficulty has been enlarged to include levels that were considered unattainable 20 years ago and tough routes are no longer the prerogative of a few top climbers.

The introduction of regulations and safety criteria has done nothing to detract from the appeal of this sport; it is the psychological aspect that makes it so different to so many others. All they have done is to make it accessible to all. Climbing is now seen as a test of physical, technical, and mental ability, carried out in totally safe conditions, so as to get the best possible performance from whoever is practicing it, regardless of surroundings.

Nowadays completely freed from its mountaineering origins, climbing has become a fully recognized sporting activity, which ought to have a place in the Olympics. Perhaps one day it will.

Sport climbing is mainly practiced on rock walls of moderate height (left) or on artificial structures (above).

KEY DATES

First years of the 20th century: James William Puttrell is recorded as the first man in the world to have scaled a rock wall purely for its own sake, without any protection at all, on the gritstone of England's Peak District.

1910: German Hans Kresz invents the first soft climbing shoe with a felt sole.

1918: On the sandstone pillars near Dresden, East Germany a successful free climbing ascent of the western edge of Wilder Kopf makes this the first sixth grade climb in history.

1957–1958: The granite rock faces of the Yosemite valley (USA) are conquered. On June 28, 1957 Robbins, Gallwas and Sherrick reach the summit of Half Dome, and just over a year later,

Lynn Hill in action.

on November 12, 1958, Harding, backed up by Merry, successfully climbs the legendary Nose route on the 1000m (3280 feet) high granite mass El Capitan. Over the following years many climbers are to attempt to climb the Nose without support (freestyle), but it is not until 1993 that someone succeeds …. and that someone is a woman: the American Lynn Hill, a climber in a class of her own, who is unmatched to this day.

1968: The first limestone routes of the Verdon gorges (France) are opened up, and soon become (and still are) a cult site for climbers from all around the world. The most famous route is La Demande, the longest in the main sector L'Escalès, covering 300m (984 feet) of large and impressive fissures. The first to climb it are François Guillot and Joel Coqueugniot, thus becoming climbing legends. Today there are more than 900 routes in the Verdon gorges.

1000 granite meters of the Nose.

1970: Magnesite is used for the first time in Colorado. Over the next few years many arguments arise over whether or not leaving white powder prints on the rocks was ethical.

Structure for the first World Cup in Leeds (England).

Bouldering with magnesite.

1985: In Bardonecchia, (Italy), SportRoccia 85 is organized, the first international sport climbing competition, in which almost all the leading climbers of the time compete against each other. This is the start of sport climbing as a competitive sport, becoming truly recognized as a sport in its own right.

1989: The first official round of the sport climbing World Cup took place in Leeds (England).

1999: The first official Bouldering World Cup. For the competition rock masses are replaced by resin structures of about three meters (ten feet) in height. Today

there are three areas of competition in sport climbing and three international circuits: Difficulty (the most traditional of the competitions, on high structures with ropes), Speed (which has also existed for several years) and Bouldering.

First round of the World Cup in Milan (Italy).

2
MATERIALS AND EQUIPMENT

Personal equipment and equipment for progression and safety. How to fit out a route.

Personal equipment

Harness

An essential piece of equipment is the belt with thigh straps (the harness), by which the climber is attached to the rope and to which he attaches various pieces of equipment useful for the climb. In the case of a fall, it is designed to spread the force of the impact between the climber's legs and back. It is usually made of polyamide or polyester fiber of a suitable thickness with ultra-resistant stitching, guaranteed to support forces of 16 kilo Newtons, and with lightly padded inserts for increased comfort.

When you put the harness on, it is crucial that the fastening tape is passed twice inside the buckle so as to block it, otherwise, when subjected to pressure, there is a risk of it slipping round and causing the harness itself to open.

Shoes

Shoes must be close-fitting and the soles should consist of a special mix of rubber, which give your feet excellent grip on rock or resin. There are different types of shoes, for every type of rock and every type of climber: more or less rigid, with or without insoles, laced, with Velcro fastening, without laces (ballerina style). The ballerina style shoe, without insole, is the softest and most comfortable to wear. Contrary to what one might think, it is the least suitable for a beginner, because it does not support the foot, and does not easily stay where it is planted unless the climber has already mastered excellent footwork

BELT

CIRCULAR STRAP
JOINING BELT TO
THIGH STRAPS

THIGH STRAPS

RING FOR ATTACHING
EQUIPMENT

METAL BUCKLE

techniques. Those who are just starting climbing will certainly be more at ease with a laced shoe, which binds the foot better, and makes it easier to distribute weight.

is clipped onto the back of the harness with a small karabiner, or hung by a string attached to the climber's waist.

Magnesite and magnesite-bag

Climbers, like gymnasts, use magnesium powder to absorb the sweat from their hands and provide the best possible grip. Magnesite is kept in a little bag, large enough to allow a hand to be inserted, that

UIAA AND CEN REGULATIONS

The UIAA (Union Internationale des Associations d'Alpinisme) has produced a set of regulations, valid all over the world, which sets out the minimum requisites that must be satisfied before its symbol can be used. These regulations have subsequently been acknowledged, and partly modified, by the Comité Européen de Normalisation (European Committee for Standardization – CEN) and no product is allowed to be marketed without the CEN mark. The presence of this symbol, together with that of the UIAA, on any product that is bought, is sure indication of its safety and quality, which is of fundamental importance for anyone practicing this sport.

The symbol UIAA cannot be used on lower body harnesses (though they do have the CEN mark), as they are not considered safe enough for long falls in a mountain environment. These regulations, however, only envisage the sort of situation that is encountered in mountaineering; they only take into account the possibility of a long fall with an upper body harness (i.e. one that also has shoulder straps). This spreads the impact over the upper back as well, thus avoiding the spine being dangerously bent, and preventing the climber being upturned should they be carrying a rucksack on their back. It is obvious that there is a discrepancy between these regulations and the everyday reality of climbing; they seem to be completely ignoring the use of the lower body harness in sport climbing, in which falls are shorter and almost totally free of risk. Nor do people practice sport climbing with weights on their shoulders, and the use of the upper body harness has been obsolete for years now, because it was uncomfortable and impractical.

Progression and safety equipment

Rope

All climbing ropes are slightly elastic, so as to withstand strong pressures and to partly absorb the impact of a fall, which would otherwise be totally taken by the climber.

For practical sport climbing, the ropes on the market go from 50 to 70 meters in length, with a diameter that varies from 9·4 to 10·5 millimeters. Until a few years ago, ropes with an 11 millimeter diameter were still in use, considered safer than those of a smaller diameter. Then ropes that were equally safe but thinner were successfully produced, with a diameter of less than 10 millimeters, which have the advantage of being much lighter and much more

On ropes that have been certified you will find a label that tells you its length, its diameter, and whether it is for use as a single rope (1) or as a pair ($\frac{1}{2}$).

HOW THE ROPE IS MADE

The rope, the equipment to which a climber entrusts his life, is made of very thin nylon fibers (60 to 70 thousand) entwined according to a very precise scheme. The interior section, known as the core, is designed to support and absorb the impact of a fall. The outer part, known as the casing, is a thick tube of material designed to resist abrasion and rubbing, and it also serves the purpose of protecting the core from the harmful action of UV rays, which would make it deteriorate prematurely.

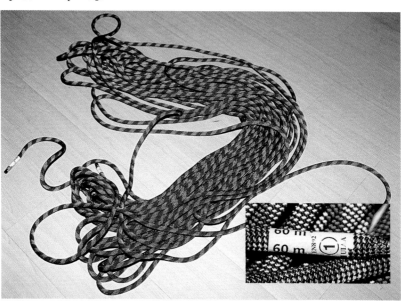

manageable, but are equally resistant. They should carry the symbol UIAA, as well as the symbol (1) to indicate that they can be used as a single rope. Then there is the symbol ($\frac{1}{2}$), found on half ropes, of an 8 to 9 millimeter diameter, which must be used in pairs, and are purely for mountaineering use.

Rope should be replaced every two to three years, depending on how often you go climbing (even every year if necessary). It should also be checked frequently, and always after any accident that might have damaged it, to make sure that the outer casing is intact and that there are no areas that appear softer (i.e. where the core has become frayed); that there are no abrasions or parts of the core showing through the casing; and that there are no swollen sections or irregularities in thickness which would indicate damage to the interior. Trampling the rope with your feet should at all costs be avoided.

Cords

Cords (thin ropes) are made of the same material and in the same way as ropes, but obviously they are of a smaller diameter (6 to 7 millimeters). They are used for securing yourself or for descents, after first being knotted to form a ring.

Karabiners

A karabiner is a lightweight, highly resistant, metal ring, with a hinged (snap-gate) or screwgate security opening, which is used in most maneuvers involving a rope.

In sport climbing especially, opening karabiners, with a hinged lever, are used for advancing, i.e. to secure oneself to the safety points found on a route in the course of a climb, while screwgate karabiners are used to join the descender to the harness

Hingegate (or snapgate) karabiners for progression (1,2).

Screwgate karabiners for linking the descender to the harness (3).

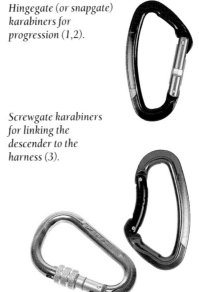

when attaching a partner. All karabiners should be able to withstand a load of at least 22 kilo Newtons (kN) vertically, and 7kN sideways (6kN sideways if the lever is open).

Quick-draws

The quick-draw is a piece of equipment composed of two karabiners linked by a circular strap sewn together in the middle; one of the karabiners is attached to the bolt, while the rope to which the climber is attached is passed through the other.

It can be bought already made up, but you can also put it together yourself by buying a strap and karabiners separately (the strap must support a minimum load of 22kN).

If you wish to be completely self-sufficient when you go climbing, it is recommended that you have a set of at least twelve quick-draws.

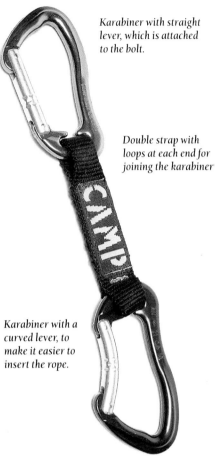

Karabiner with straight lever, which is attached to the bolt.

Double strap with loops at each end for joining the karabiner

Karabiner with a curved lever, to make it easier to insert the rope.

Descenders

This is a piece of equipment that allows you to ensure the safety of your roped partner, and to make descending and retrieval maneuvers.

Their purpose is to stop the rope running through with a minimum effort on

Left: a correctly positioned quickdraw.

24

the part of the belayer or during a controlled descent. They are made with the same light alloys used for karabiners, and support loads greater than 20kN. The most commonly used in climbing are:
- Figure of eight
- Sticht belay plate.[f6]

Self-blocking security systems

This is a mechanical system for ensuring the safety of your roped partner. Its purpose is to block the rope automatically if it is subjected to a sudden jerk, i.e. in case the climber falls. The most commonly used are:
- Gri-gri
- Yo -yo

Figure of eight descender.

Gri-gri open and closed.

Yo-yo.

Sticht belay plate.

Route equipment

On routes that are fitted out in accordance with sport climbing criteria, you will find bolts to guarantee safety in case of a fall and to facilitate a trouble-free descent once the belay point has been reached.

These bolts are set into holes in the rock that have been previously trepanned, and belong essentially to one of two types:
• Expansion bolts
• Resin (screw-in) bolts.

Expansion bolts

These are expanding or pressure bolts, which are inserted into holes that have been previously made at a suitable point in the rock face. A plate with a hole in it is then screwed to the outer end of the bolt. These were the first sort of bolts to be used on rock walls and are still among the best type of anchorage in use today. The old versions were fixed with 8 millimeter bolts and tended to oxidize over time. Nowadays bolts with a diameter of 10 to 12 millimeters are used, made of stainless steel or other equally resistant alloys, and are altogether safer and longer lasting. They can withstand loads of at least 26kN. On some cliffs that have not been re-equipped for years it is still possible to find 8 millimeter bolts, easily recognizable because of their small size and old appearance (as they

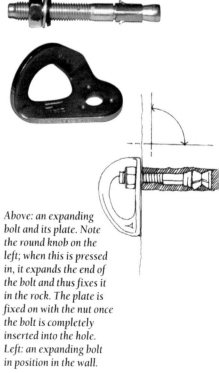

Above: an expanding bolt and its plate. Note the round knob on the left; when this is pressed in, it expands the end of the bolt and thus fixes it in the rock. The plate is fixed on with the nut once the bolt is completely inserted into the hole. Left: an expanding bolt in position in the wall.

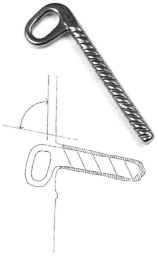

Above: a screw-in bolt, made from a solid cast piece of steel. It is inserted into a hole made in the rock and fixed in place by a suitable epoxy glue.
Left: a screw-in bolt fixed in the rock face.

oxidize they turn a dark brownish color). It is advisable to check their strength before entrusting your safety to them, or else to avoid climbing on walls with this sort of equipment altogether.

Resin bolts (screw-in bolts)

These are high resistance bolts, made of a single cast piece of stainless steel or carbon alloy, which are fixed to the rock by a special resin (epoxy glue), in previously prepared holes. Screw-in bolts are also 10 to 12 millimeters in diameter, and can resist loads of between 30 and 35kN. The larger ones are particularly recommended for very soft rock, such as certain types of limestone.

Belays (stopping points)

A belay is the term used for the end of a climbing section either at the summit or on the wall. Before explaining what exactly a belay consists of, it is necessary to digress a little first.

The "field of action" in sport climbing is made up of single pitches, i.e. routes that are only one piece of rope long, with the possibility of securing yourself at the base. The development of single pitch routes is limited by the standard length of the climbing ropes currently on the market, which range, as has been described, from 50 to 70 meters in length. At the end of each rope length on the wall a belay point is incorporated, from which climbers can lower themselves or be lowered down by their belayer in complete safety.

There are also many rock walls on which multi-pitch routes have been laid out in accordance with sport climbing criteria, where it is possible to complete some amazingly beautiful climbs in complete safety. On long routes fitted with bolts according to sport climbing criteria, each pitch is usually not more than 30 to 35 meters in length, and ends at a belay point where the leader can stop to secure themself and recover their partner, and from which their partner will belay them for the next stretch.

Modern belays consist of two fixed points (spits or screw-in bolts) linked by a piece of chain. They are usually made of stainless steel or other high resistance alloys and can support loads of minimum 20kN. Clipped onto one of the two fixed points is a descent karabiner, or a high resistance metal ring with a quick opening latch, or a soldered ring, through which the rope must be passed for descending (see 3, Safety Techiques) or, in the case of multi-pitch routes, to which you must attach yourself to then bring up your partner.

Left: single pitch routes (one rope length) mean that the belayer can stand at the bottom of the wall.
Below: Belay points consist of expanding or screw-in bolts linked to a karabiner by a length of chain with a soldered ring (1) or a descent karabiner (2).

3
SAFETY
TECHNIQUES AND
MANEUVERS

Types of knots for attaching yourself and for rope maneuvers. Security and descent techniques.

KNOTS
For attaching yourself
Figure-of-eight knot

This is the most traditional knot. Make sure you check carefully that you have completely threaded the end of the rope back through.

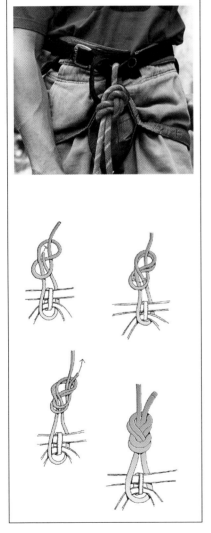

Bowline on the bight

Also frequently used, this knot offers the advantage of never pulling itself tight, even after one or more falls, and it is thus very quick to undo, and does less damage to the rope. It is, however, not very safe if not properly threaded through, as it tends to undo itself. It is therefore important always to thread it through and to make a security knot at the end of the rope as a precaution.

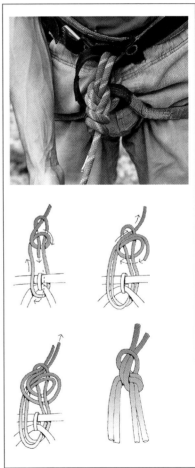

What to avoid
The knot is done. Avoid any distraction while you are attaching yourself, always finish the knot, and check it again (1)

Typical beginners' mistakes: the rope is passed through only one of the points of the harness. Avoid this, or risk being held only by the thigh straps (and being upended) or only by the belt (ribcage squashed and difficulty breathing) (2).

Except when climbing as second, where this practice is tolerated even though it is not correct, you must under no circumstances attach yourself to a karabiner, even one with a screwgate opening, because if it turns sideways (as often happens), a karabiner can rarely support more than 800kg (1764 pounds), and this is likely to be insufficient in the event of a fall (3).

Avoid attaching yourself by the strap that joins the two sections of the harness. Although it may be strong, it is not reinforced as the two attachment points are, and anyway it is always better to be attached at two points rather than at one (4).

Knots for rope maneuvers

Half clove hitch

This is basically a security knot. Easy to do and very safe, but it does have the drawback of wearing out the rope. However, it is important to know how to do it, in case you ever find yourself without mechanical safety devices.

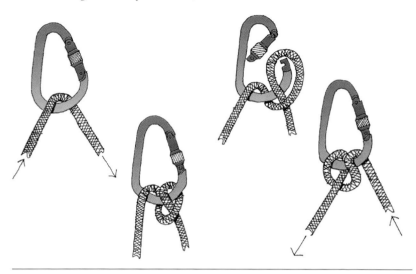

Clove hitch

An extremely important knot, always used for securing oneself at a stopping point. As well as being totally safe, it allows you to increase or reduce the length of the rope between yourself and the anchor point without undoing it. It is always best to attach it to a screwgate karabiner, which is not likely to open, and it is important to learn how to tie it straight onto a karabiner with only one hand.

Joining knots

Tape knot

This is used to join straps. It is the only safe knot for this type of material, but there is a risk of it coming undone if it is not perfectly executed.

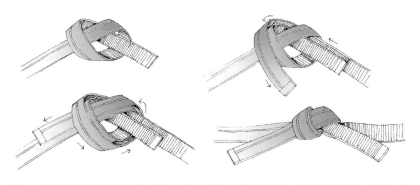

Single or double Fisherman's bend

This is used to make a rope ring or to link two ropes. The single one is quicker to do, but it slips a little and it is difficult to undo after it has been pulled hard. The double one (3) is bulky but preferable, and it allows ropes of different diameters to be joined.

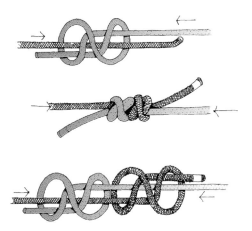

Sheet bend

This is used to join two ropes of the same diameter. It is preferable to the Fisherman's knot when rappelling.

Self-blocking security knots

Prusik knot

This is used to secure yourself when rappelling, in emergency maneuvers, for re-ascending, and for retrieval. It slips both ways and can be blocked by a strong tug downwards. It is always done with a cord that is much smaller in diameter than the rope.

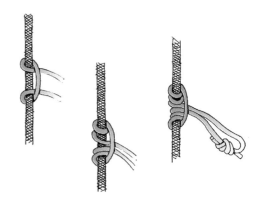

Kleimheist

This serves the same purpose as the Prusik, but has the advantage of sliding better in both directions. It is easy to adjust (depending on how many times the rope is wound round) and it is effective even in difficult conditions, when the rope is wet or muddy.

Locking loop

This is an emergency knot, for securing the rope at the anchor point so that you can proceed in safety to other maneuvers. It is always finished off with a counter knot for safety.

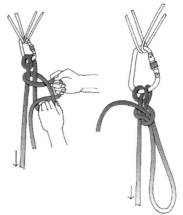

SECURITY METHODS AND TECHNIQUES

Here is a brief overview of the most commonly used safety devices, and some advice on their correct use. You should bear in mind that in sport climbing falls are frequent, and are not considered a major accident as they would be in mountaineering.

Figure of eight

This is the most common descender, which you need to know how to use right from the start, as it is also the piece of equipment that is most often used for rappelling (double rope descents) from belay points. A loop or rope is passed through the larger hole and then around the smaller one, which is then joined to the harness by a screwgate karabiner. It is very important, when belaying your partner, that you always link the descender to your harness with a screwgate karabiner, which is not likely to open, and also, obviously, that you remember to shut the screwgate.

The braking action of the figure of eight is provided by the friction of the rope on it,

Left: the correct way to attach the rope to the figure of eight descender.
Above: the correct stance for belaying your partner with a figure of eight descender.

and so it is important that the section of the rope that goes to the belayer forms as acute an angle as possible with the rope that is entering the brake. It is also essential that the belayer never slackens their hold on the part of the rope that is feeding into the figure of eight, and keeps it held tight from below. You should alternate the hand with which you are holding the rope, so as never to let go, either when you are securing a partner climbing on a top rope, or when you are feeding rope to the leader. Finally, when lowering your partner, hold the rope downwards with both hands and let it slip through. The disadvantage of the figure of eight is that it gets the ropes twisted and causes them to overheat in long descents.

Below: the belayer should never let go of the rope, taking only one hand off at a time, when securing their partner when top-roping (1,2,3,4), when giving rope to their partner (5), or when lowering them (6).

Sticht belay plate

This is a safety device that works in a manner similar to the figure of eight. You insert a loop of the rope, which is then attached by a screwgate karabiner to your harness. Once again, the belayer must never let go of the rope that is feeding in. As with the figure of eight, the sharper the angle formed by the rope held by the belayer and the rope entering the equipment, the less effort they will have to make to stop their partner. Compared to the figure of eight, the plate twists the rope less, but gets equally overheated.

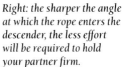

Left: the correct way to insert the rope loop into the sticht plate and attach it to the karabiner. Above: once again, the belayer should never let go of the rope that comes out of the sticht plate towards them.

Right: the sharper the angle at which the rope enters the descender, the less effort will be required to hold your partner firm.

Gri-gri

The Gri-gri (Petzl) is a self-locking safety device, consisting of a mechanism that blocks the rope when it is pulled sharply, i.e. whenever your partner falls or is hanging. It is a completely safe and practical piece of equipment, highly valued by climbers, that has now almost completely supplanted the more traditional systems just described (figure of eight and Sticht plate). However, it needs to be used with care and demands a certain level of expertise, especially in inserting the rope correctly, as clearly instructed on the mechanism. It is also a good rule never to let go of the section of rope that comes out of it towards you when you are belaying. (If the rope is new, or does not create any friction during the ascent, and the climber is not heavy enough, it can happen that the gri-gri only blocks the cord after a fall of several meters.)

Above: the correct way to insert the rope into the gri-gri is explained on the mechanism.
Left: when belaying the leader, you should always let the rope out in a controlled manner, to ensure that it runs easily, and to avoid sudden jerks which might block it. It is also a good rule never to let go of the rope that comes out towards you, to prevent it stopping only after your partner has already fallen.

When belaying the leader in a roped party, always help the rope along, easing its exit from the gri-gri, and avoiding any sudden tugs which would block the equipment, and make your partner's climb difficult.

You will need to familiarize yourself with giving rope quickly to the leader when they have to attach karabiners, and – very important – you must never hold on to the part of the rope that goes towards the climber. In the event of a fall your instinctive reaction would be to tighten your grip (it has already happened to many people), thus preventing it pulling suddenly and activating the blocking system, with the result that you send your partner flying down to the ground and risk getting rope burn on your hands. It is also important not to feed the rope while keeping the friction tight with your hand, at the risk once again of forgetting to remove your hand should your partner fall. All you need is a little practice to learn how to use this system correctly.

When lowering your partner, all you need to do is pull the lever at the top to the left, and control the speed of descent.

Yo-yo

The yo-yo (Camp) is another very useful self-blocking system. You insert the rope into the correct side, as indicated, and attach the rope and the mechanism to the screwgate karabiner that is attached to the central strap of your harness. It has a double braking system; when the rope is pulled sharply it makes the yo-yo swivel round the karabiner and jams against the karabiner itself in a V shape. With the yo-yo, as with the gri-gri, it is best not to let go of the section of the rope that is feeding in and to help the rope along when belaying the leader, so as to avoid the rope blocking.

To lower your partner all you need to do is to pull the upper part of the mechanism slowly towards you.

Insert the rope correctly into the yo-yo (1,2).

When the rope is pulled, it is gripped tight by the mechanism (3).

By pulling the mechanism towards your body you can lower your partner (4).

MANEUVERS AT A BELAY
Belays with an opening karabiner
If the belay is fitted with a hingegate or a screwgate karabiner, suitably positioned for the descent, all you have to do is open the karabiner at the belay and pass the rope into it without untying yourself, check that the karabiner is properly closed, get your partner to block the rope, and let yourself be lowered. This is the simplest situation, and does not require any self-securing maneuvers. Often, however, the chain at the belay is not fitted with an opening karabiner, but with a soldered ring or a karabiner with a snaphook opening. It can happen that the karabiner's lever is so stiff that it no longer opens. In such cases it is necessary to attach yourself to the stopping point and untie yourself so as to pass the rope through the chain and then lower yourself.

Belay points without karabiner or with a shut karabiner
There are two equally safe methods that can be adopted in this case: lowering off or untying yourself before passing the rope through the chain.

If the belay point is already fitted with a karabiner, all you need to do is pass the rope through it (left) and let yourself be lowered by your partner (right).

First method: lowering off
This is a very quick and safe method, and there is no moment at which you need to rely solely on the quick-draw from which you are hanging, because when you untie yourself you are already attached by another knot.

As soon as you reach the belay, you attach yourself with a quick-draw to one of the two anchor points on which the chain is fixed, checking that it is in a good condition (1).

Clip a karabiner, preferably a screwgate one, onto the strap that joins the two parts of your harness (2).

Thread a long loop of the rope that is attached to your waist through the karabiner or soldered ring at the end of the chain (3).

Make a figure of eight knot with this loop (4) and attach it to the screwgate karabiner (5).

Once you are secured by a new knot, you can undo the one that you were attached by before reaching the belay point; this frees the end of the rope that needs to be passed through the ring on the chain so that you can descend (6).

Tell your partner to block the rope, and then, once you have detached and retrieved the quick-draw that you were hanging from, you can be lowered (7).

Second method: untying yourself before passing the rope through the chain

As in the previous case, you attach yourself to one of the two anchor points with a quick-draw. To the other anchor point you attach a karabiner, or another quick-draw, to which you tie yourself with an ordinary knot, or better still a bowline, which allows you to adjust the length of the piece of rope with which you are working (1,2,3).

After securing the rope, you untie yourself, pass the end of the rope through the ring of the chain, and attach yourself at the harness again (4,5). At this point you undo the bowline (6) with which you had

Once you are secured to the belay by a quick-draw, you can arrange the rope in complete safety for rappelling.

fastened the rope, retrieve the karabiner and settle yourself onto the rope (7). Only after making sure that the belayer has blocked the rope can you detach the quick-draw (8) and let yourself down (9).

Some practical advice

Both these methods are safe and quick, if you have a good grasp of the maneuvers involved. For the first few attempts you are strongly advised to have the help of an expert friend or instructor. It used to be standard good practice for climbers to secure themselves to the chain by a loop of rope attached to a screwgate karabiner, as, unlike a quick-draw, there is no risk of this opening. In practice, however, climbers on a cliff no longer carry spare ropes or straps,

but only the bare essentials, so as to be as light and unencumbered as possible: the correct number of quickdraws for bolts on the route, and a couple extra for maneuvers at belays.

A quick-draw is completely safe anyway and is not likely to open if you lean on it with all your weight and if the karabiners are not touched at all during maneuvers. Always check knots after tying them and make sure that your partner has blocked the rope before detaching the quick-draw with which you have attached yourself.

Rappelling (double rope descent)

If the belay point is such that a descent controlled from the base is not possible (e.g. belay points on ropes without a karabiner), or if you need to descend the rock face after having completed a multi-pitch route, you will need to be able to lower yourself down, which means rappelling. The sequence of movements to be carried out may be summarized as follows:

– Secure yourself at the belay.

– Untie yourself and run the rope through the descent ring until you reach the midpoint. If you are descending on two ropes, you must join them with a sheet bend and then run one of the ropes through the descent ring until you reach the joining knot. (A)

– Retrieve the two ends and make a knot at the end of each one, in case they do not reach the ground, and then throw them out wide of the rock face, to avoid them getting caught on some projecting rock or bush

For rappelling with two ropes, the link knot should be positioned just below the belay ring (A).

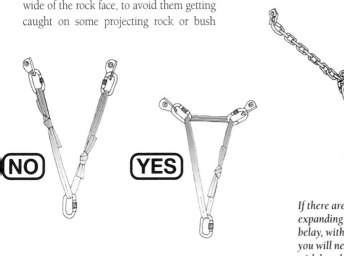

NO: If one bolt comes out the karabiner can slip off.

YES: The karabiner remains attached to the strap if one bolt comes out.

If there are only expanding bolts at the belay, without a chain, you will need to fit them with karabiners and a strap.

(which would entail having to disentangle the rope while descending).

– Make a Kleimheist or Prusik knot with a loop of rope on both the ropes, and attach it to your harness with a screwgate karabiner.

– Attach another rope loop to the fastening of your harness with a tight knot or with a karabiner.

– Fit a descender on to the ropes above the self-locking knot, fix it to a screwgate

It is common practice to use only one hand to control the descent when being lowered by a descender (B), but it is safer to also use a self-locking knot attached to a screwgate karabiner that is fixed to your harness (C), which you accompany with a hand while descending (D).

karabiner, and attach the latter to the second rope loop. (B)

– Lower yourself down, keeping a hold of the self-locking knot with one hand and controlling the speed of descent with the other, which should be holding the rope at hip height. (C)

Although it is possible (and many are in the habit of doing this) to rappel using only the descender (D), it is always best to also make a self-locking knot as a guarantee of safety during the descent, since for a variety of reasons (descending too quickly, feeling ill, exhaustion) it can happen that you let go of the rope with both hands. A mishap of this sort can have dramatic consequences if you have not made a self-locking knot. A Kleimheist or Prusik knot, on the other hand, if not guided, will pull tight on the ropes, thus preventing the climber from plummeting down. All that you then need to do is slide the knot upwards a little to unblock it, and then you can carry on the descent.

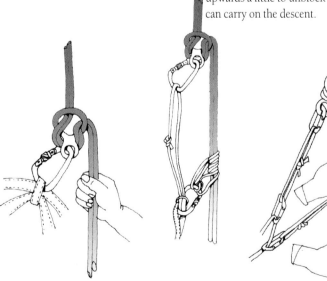

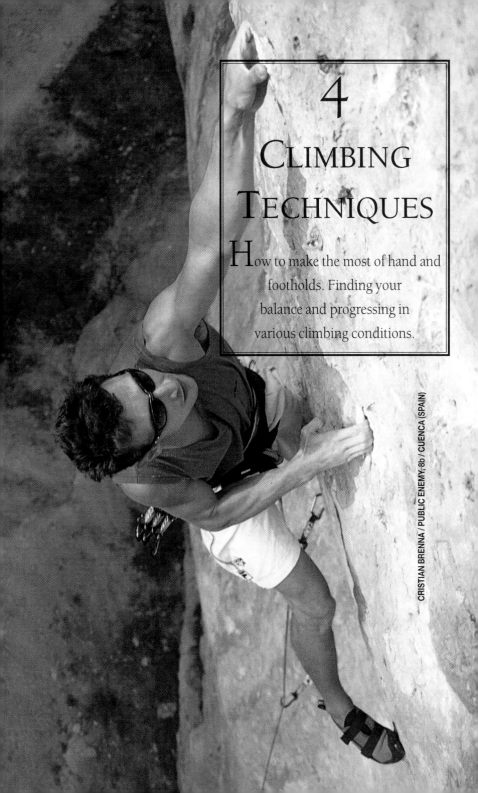

4

CLIMBING
TECHNIQUES

Ⓗow to make the most of hand and
footholds. Finding your
balance and progressing in
various climbing conditions.

TAKING THE FIRST STEPS

When you watch a highly experienced climber making his way up a route without any apparent effort, you get the impression that climbing is an easy sport, born of spontaneous movements. Climbing is in fact an innate instinct in children, but their co-ordination of movement is fairly poor and basic. Similarly, a beginner's first attempt at a wall with large and obvious hand and footholds is usually straightforward and enjoyable. Problems arise as soon as there is a handhold too distant to reach, or one that is difficult to use because it is vertical or slanting rather than horizontal.

Beginners usually look for horizontal handholds like "handles" since they do not have enough experience to think of more imaginative solutions. Their behavior reveals a very ad hoc sense of balance and

co-ordination; these abilities need to be gradually developed by training. To be successful at climbing you need to be aware of your own body, you need to learn how to feel, move, and co-ordinate your movements, how to balance and how to position yourself correctly. Obviously it is only by practical experience that you can make real progress, but it is also useful to have grasped the theory.

HANDHOLDS AND FOOTHOLDS

It is important, when you begin climbing, to learn how to recognize the different types of hand and footholds, so as to be able to locate them on the rock face and make use of them to progress. For many people, their first experience of climbing is on artificial walls, which can now be found in gyms in cities all around the world. Here the approach is much simpler, since the environment factor is missing, and the chunks of resin that serve as hand and footholds are colorful and obvious.

On real rock the matter becomes more complicated, since the natural rock wall is more homogeneous, rarely offering obvious protuberances, and it is not easy to distinguish good, or at least useful holds from useless ones.

The learning process must be gradual, always starting from easy and progressing to more difficult, but in climbing nothing is commonplace, and it requires intelligent use of movement and concentration.

Handholds

Handholds are projections or cavities that may be more or less marked, either natural or artificial, which you grasp in order to progress.

Your fingers need to adapt themselves to the rock or the resin, so as to get the most out of the shape of the handhold. They can be extended or curled; with extended fingers your forearm will get less tired, whereas with flexed fingers you can apply greater force to the handhold, especially if it is a small and sharp-edged one. Sometimes it is necessary to place your thumb on top of the other fingers to increase your grip.

The best way to make use of a handhold lies in identifying the best angle to weight it from. A handhold can usually be used in several ways, among which some (sometimes only one) are the optimal ones. The further away you get from this, the less effective will be the manner in which you can use that particular handhold for progression.

Jug or bucket
This is the easiest handhold to use, since your whole hand fits into it. It is grasped like the rung of a ladder.

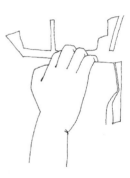

Crimp (notch)
This is a horizontal and sharp-edged handhold, varying in size from a few centimeters to a few millimeters wide (a mini-crimp). Only the first joints of your fingers or your fingertips fit into it. The pressure applied by your thumb reinforces the grip of the other fingers.

Sidepull

This is a vertical handhold, usually sharp-edged like the crimp, and in order to use it, sideways pressure must be applied; it would be useless to try to apply downward pressure to it.

Sloper

This is a very elusive hold that must be used with your hand in maximum contact with its surface.

Pinch

This handhold needs to be grasped with your thumb on the opposite side to the other fingers. A very easily distinguishable type of pinch hold, which is found on limestone rock walls, is the "pipe", the shape of which is reminiscent of an organ pipe.

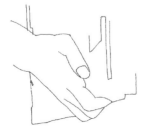

Undercut

This handhold is used with the palm of your hand above your fingers. It is very difficult to make use of it as long as it is level with your head or higher, but it becomes gradually easier the higher your feet are, when you stretch your arm downwards towards it.

Pocket

If your whole hand does not go in, it can also be called a one-finger, two-finger, or three-finger pocket, according to the number of fingers that can be inserted. To use it effectively you need a lot of experience; you have to learn the best way of inserting your fingers, which depends on the way the hole is formed.

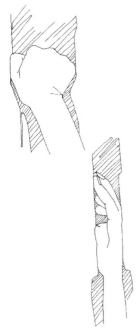

Fissure (jamming)

This type of handhold can vary greatly in size, and so the way that it is used is equally varied. Some fissures lend themselves to being used with sideways pressure, with a side pull, while you can jam your hand or fingers into others. With these latter, depending on the size of the fissure, you insert your fingers, your whole hand or your fist, and then make a twisting movement so as to increase the pressure.

Footholds

Footholds are really the same thing as handholds, but are used instead by the feet, which transfer the weight of your body to the hold. Often while climbing the same hold will be used first by your hands, then by your feet, while at other times it may work out easier to use a smaller foothold, which could not be used as a handhold but which is better positioned for the movement that you wish to make. In any case, every projection and every cavity can be either a handhold or a foothold.

Correct footing is essential if you are to make progress in sport climbing. Beginners (and not only beginners) often do not trust their feet, or rather they do not think that they can entrust their weight to a foothold, which may be very small indeed. The result is that they do not put enough weight on it, or push hard enough with their foot, and this is precisely why their foot slips away. The smaller the foothold, the more you need to weight it, in order to concentrate the greatest load possible on that point and to get maximum grip from your climbing shoe. Using your feet is certainly less instinctive than using your hands and you will need to go through a long learning period to acquire the correct technique and be able to apply it automatically.

To start with, let's look at the different types of foothold.

Step or ledge

This is the easiest foothold to make use of, as the jug is for hands. Sharp-edged and well defined, you apply your weight to it with the front part of your shoe.

Notch

This is a sharp-edged foothold, either horizontal or slanting. It only supports the very tip of your toes, with the weight on either the inside or the outside toe edges, depending on the type of movement that you are making.

Pocket

Holes are not easy to weight in the correct way, as they do not offer a flat surface and only the tip of your shoe fits in.

Smearing

This involves planting your foot on a section of the wall that offers neither projections nor cavities, and relies entirely on the friction between the sole and the rock (or artificial wall).

It can be done on slanting sections of the wall (in which case the whole base of the foot is planted), but also on very demanding vertical walls (in which case only the tip of the foot is planted).

Jamming

A foot can be jammed into a fissure; depending on the width of the latter, it may be the entire foot or only the toes.

In small or medium size fissures you have to insert your foot sideways and then twist it to try and straighten it again.

In wider fissures you need to jam your foot by setting the heel and the toe opposite each other.

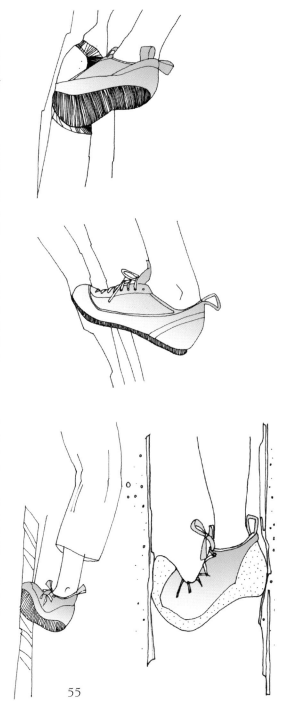

BASIC MOVEMENTS

In sport climbing, as is the case with most sports, an effort is now being made to include the range of basic movements in the teaching process, giving each a precise name, so as to create a common language, which is extremely important in the sporting and competitive environment. It is necessary to distinguish between the concept of "technique" and that of "basic movements." Technique is based on the basic movements that make it up, while a basic movement is a single movement. It is very important to learn and really absorb these basic movements in order to build up a stock of information to use in the various climbing techniques. It is equally important, if you are to be able to perform these

automatically, that you deliberately try them out in various situations under the guidance of an expert friend or, even better, of an instructor.

However, it is not possible to talk of basic movements without bringing in three essential aspects of the learning phase: finding your balance, moving your feet independently, and breathing.

Finding your balance and shifting your weight

Climbing is above all a matter of sensations and emotions. The sensory receptors of your hands, feet and eyes take in the external information, and the internal reaction that is sparked off means that you are continually adapting to the situation. As a climber you must learn how to shift the weight of your body on the rock wall in a constant search for balance. A movement that is made off balance, even if it is successful, is extremely wasteful in terms of energy and exhausts your energy reserves more quickly.

Below: how to plant your foot:
1 – front on (with your toe).
2 – on the inside edge.
3 – on the outside edge

The importance of footing

Feet should not be seen as an optional extra, to be placed wherever they can. They are equal in importance to your hands and arms. How well you use them determines how successful a movement or a series of movements will be.

When you begin climbing, to a certain

extent you will have to begin "reasoning with your feet," which means always searching for a foothold before a handhold, and then adapting the position of your torso according to how your foot is positioned on the foothold. Feet, therefore, are not appendages that follow the body, but the starting point of every movement.

From the description of the various types of footholds you will have seen how, when you are progressing, it is the front part of the shoe that is mostly used (below).

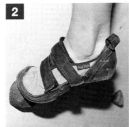

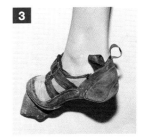

Breathing

When climbing you must not forget to breathe. It may seem a silly thing to say, but in fact climbers always hold their breath when doing the most intense sections, and when beginners are concentrating on their movements they forget to breathe regularly. Muscles need oxygen, and so you must learn to "listen" to the air that is entering and leaving your lungs, and to keep your breathing as regular as possible. Besides, thinking about your breathing also helps you to maintain concentration and self-control.

Right: on very demanding stretches you tend naturally to hold your breath, while in fact it is precisely during such movements that your muscles need more oxygen.

FRONTAL PROGRESSION

The movements involved in frontal progression are the first basic movements to be learnt, and also the simplest and easiest, which a beginner can perform in a fairly instinctive manner.

You start off in a basic position, with your body facing the wall, your legs wide apart, and your feet firmly planted on footholds. Your arms should be extended, your pelvis tilted back, and your head and shoulders held clear of the wall to give you better visibility and to be better able to plot the best route.

Left: the first movements to learn are those made with your body facing the wall, keeping your head wide so that you can better spy out hand and footholds.

Vertical shift

This is a frontal movement in an upwards direction, which is performed by putting your weight on the available foothold with the foot opposite the hand with which you are pulling on the handhold. The arm that is making use of the handhold must always be opposite the leg that is pushing, so that the vertical line of your center of gravity falls between your feet as much as possible, thus maintaining balance.

Right: during vertical shifts your weight is on the foot opposite the hand that is grasping the handhold.

Lateral shift

This is a frontal movement that is made in order to reach for a handhold located to the side, involving shifting the whole weight of your body in that direction.

In both of these shifting movements it is the lower limbs that do most of the work. The arms operate only for the foothold that is taking the weight.

Left: in sideways shifts your weight is mostly on your legs.

Changing hands

It often happens that you need to use the same handhold for both hands. If there is not enough space to put them together, you will have to slowly raise the fingers of one hand to make way for the other.

It is vital that you think ahead for this movement, leaving a space free on the handhold for the fingers that are carrying out the changeover.

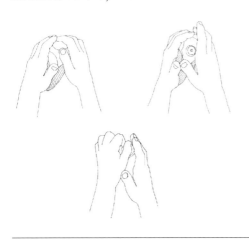

Changing feet

As with your hands, your feet will also sometimes have to use a single foothold in order to progress. One foot has already reached this spot, which now needs to support the other foot. Once again, one foot will need to gradually make space for the other on the foothold.

Crossing hands over

Sometimes in order to progress it is more convenient to reach for the next handhold by crossing over rather than by a change of hands. Crossing your hands over can be done in one of two ways:

1. With the hand that is crossing passing over the other, if the handhold to be reached is located higher than the stationary hand;

2. With the hand that is crossing passing under the other, if the handhold to be reached is located lower than the handhold already grasped.

Crossing feet over

This is also an alternative to changing feet.

Your foot should cross over inside the other one when the foothold to be reached is higher than the one that is supporting your weight (1).

Your foot should cross over outside the other one when the foothold to be reached is lower down than the one that is supporting your weight (2).

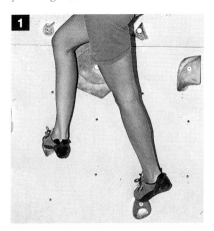

Balancing

While progressing it is usually the case that you put your weight on the opposite foot to the hand that is holding you firm, while you move towards the next handhold. If a situation occurs in which you have to push on the leg corresponding to the arm that is grasping the handhold, in order to avoid losing your balance you will then have to balance your own weight, by bringing the other leg behind the one that is supporting you (external balancing). Your body remains facing the wall and your thighs should be close together to make it easier to balance.

In internal balancing, on the other hand, your body needs to swivel from its original frontal position to a sideways one: the hand that is stretching out to reach the handhold forms a natural continuation of the leg that is crossing over. The right foot is pointed at the wall to make balancing easier. This type of balancing, besides being used when progressing, is often also used while attaching karabiners.

When you need to use hand and footholds with a hand and foot on the same side, you risk losing your balance. Right: body positioning in internal balancing. Top: positioning during external balancing.

LATERAL PROGRESSION

Performing a movement in a lateral position instead of in a frontal position makes it possible to save a lot of energy, because in sideways progression it is a question more of dynamics than of strength, and you keep your arms much more outstretched. Lateral progression is often indispensable on walls that jut out a lot.

Sideways weighting

This is ideal when you need to use a vertical handhold that is most effective if pulled from the side. It is a very useful movement, often indispensable, when climbing on overhangs, because it involves less effort than frontal clamping and it allows you to make the best use of your own weight.

You weight your foot on its outside edge and your body will find itself in the lateral position, with your hip clinging to the wall; in this way you can make use of the whole length of your body and reach very high handholds. The hand that is clamped is opposite the leg that is pushing; the other arm is stretched towards the handhold you wish to reach, while the other leg is extended into space, or has its toes against the wall to balance the weight.

For this basic movement to be really effective it is very important that you push hard on the load-bearing leg.

Sideways weighting often allows you to make better use of a vertical hold, especially on overhanging stretches, with less waste of energy.

Egyptian movement

The Egyptian is another lateral movement that is used in order to be able to stretch the body better towards the handhold, and it also expends less energy than external weighting.

To perform the Egyptian your body must be turned sideways with both feet on footholds and the rear one higher up than the front one.

By putting your weight on the rear foothold and pushing with the foot on the front foothold, lower down, it is possible to get the arm that is touching the wall very high up with minimal effort. Clearly the positioning of footholds on the wall does not always allow you to perform an Egyptian.

MORE ADVANCED BASIC MOVEMENTS
Foot to hand

Sometimes a lack of footholds forces a climber to use the same hold for their feet that they have used for their hands. The hand that is clamped on the hold must gradually make space for the foot to get a sufficient hold. In order to perform this movement you need to have a very supple pelvis.

To perform foot to hand you need to be very supple and have a lot of power in your legs to push your body up.

Foot hook

This means literally what the name suggests. On very overhanging routes it can sometimes be advantageous to hook a heel round a hold if it is too high for your toes to get a grip, always assuming that the foothold is big enough. At other times, again on overhanging walls, you may be able to do a toe hook, when in a resting position or to improve balance during progression.

Heel hook (left) and toe hook (right).

Yaniro or figure of four

Called after the person who invented it, this last basic movement is difficult to perform and goes against instinct. It is a movement that is used on overhangs, when you want to reach a handhold that is very high up, but avoid making an overly risky sudden lurch. You put one leg over the opposite arm, unloading most of your body weight onto your wrist. By pushing on your arm, with your body well bunched up, it is possible to raise your body high up to reach the desired handhold with your free hand. Once you have reached it, you can release your hold with the other hand, thus freeing your arm from the pressure of your leg, and finding yourself once more in a frontal position.

CLIMBING SITUATIONS
On slabs and vertical walls

Climbing on slabs and vertical walls demands excellent footing. Sloping slabs, so long as they are provided with good handholds, are the easiest walls to tackle; they do not require an enormous amount of training and they are the ideal terrain for beginners to make their first attempts. However, especially on granite, there may be slabs that are very nearly completely smooth and of one piece; on these it becomes necessary to use very tiny holds, and so to have great sensitivity in your feet, in order to be able to grip the wall by "smearing". This type of climbing is very demanding, even though it hardly involves the use of force, and it is perfect for refining your technique and learning to trust your own feet.

Vertical walls require an equal amount of skill in footing techniques, but also demand great strength and resistance in your fingers. It is the muscles of the forearm that do the most work. In fact, while one is as difficult as the other, a route on a vertical wall will always have smaller handholds than an overhanging route, although the movements involved are less athletic.

The most common type of progression on slabs and on vertical walls is frontal. It is very important that you manage to keep your pelvis as close as possible to the wall, so as to put most of the weight on your lower limbs. Your body should only be distanced from the rock so far as is necessary to be able to spy out footholds.

On slabs it is important to keep your body close to the wall so that you can use your feet to push, and you also need a lot of strength in your fingers so that you can make use of even the smallest handholds.

Negotiating overhangs

It must be made clear straightaway that it is not true that to negotiate an overhang all you need is to have a lot of strength in your forearms. Here again footing is of fundamental importance. Obviously it is a very athletic type of climbing, in which strength and stamina play a large part, and you need to do a lot of training not just on your fingers but also on the major muscles. But as in the case of slabs, it is essential to have acquired a good technique, so that you can climb in a way that does not waste energy on pointless effort, and always manage to keep as much weight as possible on your feet. Whether or not you use the correct technique is often the deciding factor in whether or not you are successful in getting over a particular stretch.

On overhangs there are two fundamental rules to be applied: use lateral progression as much as possible, and keep your arms extended as far as you can.

Lateral progression may be said to have been invented for overhangs. At one time most climbing was on slabs, and the difficulty of the routes was determined by the size of the handholds. Now the scope has

---

CLIFF VOCABULARY

1. **Chimney:** vertical crack in a rock wall, large enough to fit in your whole body.
2. **Dihedral or corner:** near right angle formed by two nearly vertical rock walls.
3. **Fissure:** slit in the rock that is narrower than a chimney; it may be vertical, horizontal or oblique.
4. **Rock wall:** very steep rocky surface with clearly delimited edges.
5. **Slab:** vertical or slanting section of the rock wall.
6. **Overhang:** section that juts out from the vertical line.
7. **Roof:** part of the wall that juts out horizontally.

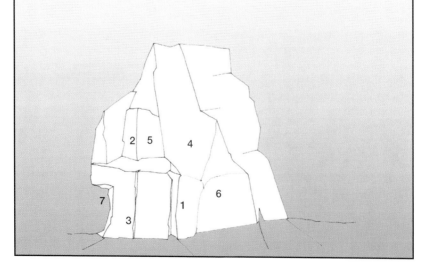

widened and new styles of climbing have arisen; sideways weighting and the Egyptian are among the key aspects in the highly evolved sport climbing of today.

A movement made in the frontal position on an overhang, especially to reach a very distant handhold, requires an enormous amount of energy to flex the arm and bring the body close to the wall. Usually the same movement, carried out in the lateral position, is far more economical and dynamic, makes better use of the push from the legs, does not involve a very great flexing of the arms, and allows you to reach handholds much further away because you are using the whole length of your body.

Clearly on an overhang there will be times when you need to flex your arms and use the major muscles, but these should be reduced to what is strictly necessary, so as to save as much energy as possible. The more you climb in the lateral position, the less strength you will waste and the more energy you will have in reserve. And even in resting positions you should grip the handholds in a relaxed manner, with your arms extended, so as to loosen your muscles and make it a real and not a pretend rest.

Right: to negotiate an overhang it is not enough just to have strong arms; it is essential to make good use of footholds.

Below: sideways weighting allows you to make better use of the thrust from your feet, and use less energy (left), while keeping your arms extended allows your muscles to rest (right).

Overcoming roofs

The same rule applies to roofs as for overhangs: use the technique that requires the least amount of energy expenditure. While you are progressing under a roof it is extremely wasteful of energy to perform a series of movements with your arms flexed; it is very important to keep them as extended as possible. You also need to have good abdominal muscles so as not to lose the grip with your feet, which you use to push your body from one handhold to another in a dynamic manner, using toe hooks and lateral movements if necessary.

However, you will not often find cliffs with horizontal routes on long naturally formed roofs, whereas they are much more common on artificial structures for training or competition (1).

On rock it is more likely that you will find small roofs on overhanging or vertical routes (2); the best way of getting over them is the foot hook, which allows you to put the weight of your body onto your leg. By pulling the hold with your heel you can raise your body out from the roof, without having to rely entirely on the pulling force of your arms, so that you can then reach for a higher handhold that allows you to raise the other leg beyond the roof as well.

In the last stage of getting over a roof the foot hook is often used.

Fissures, chimneys, and dihedrals (corners)

There are some routes, especially on granite, which follow a fissure the whole way up a smooth vertical wall; the technique for climbing these is jamming. Depending on the size of the fissure you insert either your fingers, your fist, or your arm, and then plant your feet against the vertical surface, or you can insert your toes or even your whole foot. There are also off-width fissures, which are a sort of halfway house between fissures and chimneys, into which you must insert your whole body, but which are still not big enough for you to climb by stemming (also known as bridging).

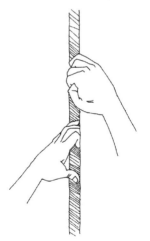

How to make use of narrow fissures (A) and wide fissures (B).
C: stemming (bridging) in a chimney; in extreme situations you may end up with your body horizontal between the walls (photo).

The way to proceed up a chimney is by stemming, in various ways that depend on the distance between the two walls: with your body against one wall and your legs against the other; in either front or side splits; or lastly, but this is a very extreme case, with your whole body horizontal between the two walls.

The dihedral, or corner, consists of two walls forming a more or less acute angle, and it may be either fissured or blank. With the former, you climb using both faces of the dihedral with your feet and the fissure with your hands, or else use the Dulfer technique. This technique (named after the Austrian mountaineer who invented it at the beginning of the 20th century) involves gripping the crack with your hands while using your legs to push away from the wall. Where there is no crack, or a crack is too narrow to be used, you climb on the two faces using opposing pressure from hands and feet, and use whatever holds the rock face may offer to help you.

In the photographs, dihedral, or corner, technique (left) and Dulfer technique (right). In the drawings, finger positioning in small fissures.

5

CLIMBING ON CLIFFS

What cliffs are. Regulations and problems. Completing a route.

FEDERICA BALTERI / MANGURRINO FREE, 7c / CUENCA (SPAIN)

CLIFFS

Sport climbing takes place on rock walls that have been fitted out for the purpose, in complete safety, without the aid of any artificial means of progression, and it is not the aim to reach a summit.

The height of the cliffs can vary from 65 or 100 feet to several hundred feet (20 or 30 to several hundred meters), but this should not be confused with the length of the routes. In fact, on cliffs of 300 feet (100m) or more in height, often only single pitch routes, of a maximum of 115 feet (35m) are fitted out (see chapter 2), or routes of two or three rope lengths (multi-pitch), which still do not reach the top of the rock wall. This is because in sport climbing the beauty of the route and the movements involved are more important

Right: cliffs in Nevada (USA) and, below, in Mallorca (Spain).

than its length. If, for example, the top part of a wall is not as interesting as the bottom part, then it is not worth the trouble of fitting it out.

The rules of the game

But if the aim of sport climbing is not to reach the top, then what is the aim? Here are three excellent objectives:

1. Enjoyment.

2. Practicing a sport that brings you into contact with nature, in unique settings, which you would be unlikely to discover in any other way.

3. Overcoming ever greater difficulties with nothing but your own strength, in continual confrontation with yourself and in a constant struggle to overcome your own limitations.

The urge to climb often leads to the discovery of amazing natural beauty spots.

WHAT CLIFFS ARE

Cliffs are rocky structures of a moderate height that may be found at any altitude, (from sea level up to the mountains), and are often just one section or the base of a slope. They may be vertical, collapsed, overhanging, sometimes actual caves. An essential feature, if they are to be climbed according to the criteria of sport climbing, is that they are equipped, in other words that someone (an Alpine guide, an expert climber), sponsored by a local authority, or a company, or using private means, has set out along logical routes the protection necessary to proceed safely.

So what counts is the difficulty of the route being tackled in relation to your limitations, the beauty of the line followed and the movements involved.

There are many aspects to sport climbing: physical, technical, and mental. And it is also a sport of course, which, like every sport, thrives on challenges; it needs objective criteria for evaluating performance and clear comprehensible rules to facilitate the challenge. Clearly its field of action, especially when it takes place on rock, is broader and more varied than that of many other sports. There are thousands of factors to take into account when determining the difficulty rating of a route, and when deciding the right and wrong way of tackling it.

There are, however, some key points, established by climbers themselves as a result of their experiences, which are central to effective climbing.

– Every route has a difficulty rating, determined by various factors.

– To successfully complete the sections you must use only the natural foot-and-handholds that the rock offers and not any artificial means.

– Completing a route means climbing up it in one go without stopping for a rest (in technical terms: without having a rest on

any of the fixed safety points) and with a rope from below, in other words, as the leader of the party. This is termed "free climbing a route."

The next few paragraphs explain what the difficulty ratings are and how they are determined, what it means to climb as leader and as second, what is meant by completing a route, and offer a few strategies for climbing in a sensible and safe manner.

Below: free climbing means climbing as leader, with a rope below you.
Below left: in sport climbing only the natural hand and footholds in the rock may be used.

Problems on the routes

On every cliff there are routes of different levels. Some cliffs have a particularly large number of easy sections, some cliffs are suitable for climbers of all levels and have a great variety of difficulty ratings, and some are "extreme" cliffs, which can only be tackled by those who have attained a very high level of expertise.

Every climber knows their own level and finds routes that are suitable for them, by getting hold of a guidebook (all the better known cliffs now have one) or by gathering information from people who are already acquainted with them. But what does the difficulty rating of a route depend on, and who determines it?

Contrary to the practice of all other

The slant of the wall is not the only factor that determines the difficulty grading of a route; this depends also on the number and size of hand and footholds.

recognized sports, in climbing there is no scientific measurement, a meter or a chronometer to measure performance. The goal that a climber is aiming for is to master a certain level of difficulty, and not just to successfully complete one route at this level.

There are various criteria that compete against one another in determining the difficulty rating of a route:
– The size and shape of the hand and footholds

– How steep the wall is

– How easy or difficult movements are

– Whether or not natural resting points occur

– Factors relating to the type of rock.

The difficulty rating is the criterion against which you measure your performance, but it is also a source of information for climbers, which gives an indication of the problems that will be encountered on an unknown route. The route is graded by the first person to make the climb without falling, who is not necessarily the person who fitted the bolts.

Having been established in this way, the grade is then officially made known to other climbers, through guidebooks or specialized magazines, or through the climbing grapevine. Giving an objective evaluation of a route is extremely difficult and requires a lot of experience. Before giving it a rating, anyone who opens up a new route generally compares it to routes that represent classic examples of a particular rating. When the route is a very demanding one, giving it a rating is tricky, and needs to be confirmed by the person who next succeeds in completing it, who often makes a slight alteration in the rating awarded. Only when a route has been completed by several climbers can its rating be considered definitive.

Below: it is only by climbing as leader that you can say you have completed a route.

The scale of difficulty ratings

The various climbing centers scattered throughout the world have worked out, over the years, different evaluation scales. In Europe the most commonly used scale is the French one, composed of numbers and letters, but in some countries, such as Germany, the mountaineering scale of the UIAA is still used, which has been extended from the sixth up to the twelfth grade. On the English scale the overall rating of a route is based on the technical difficulty (French scale) with an additional danger rating (E) since many routes in England are not fitted out and are difficult to protect. A comparison of the different systems is given below: UIAA, French, American, English (2) and Australian.

In the last ten years levels of difficulty have been reached that were once unimaginable. The highest level that has so far been confirmed is 8c+, but some climbers

Comparative table of difficulty ratings

UIAA	FRA	USA	GB Technique	GB Danger	AU
III	3	5	5.5		11
IV	4	5.6	4a		12
IV+	4	5.7			
V-	5a	5.8			13
V	5b	5.9	4b		14
V+	5c	5.10	4c		15
VI-	6a	5.10b	5a		16
VI	6a+	5.10c		E1	18
VI+	6b	5.10d	5b		19
VII-	6b	5.11a		E2	20
VII	6c	5.11b	5c		21
VII+	6c+	5.11c		E3	22
VIII-	7a	5.11d	6a		23
VIII	7a+	5.12a		E4	25
VIII+	7b	5.12b	6b		26
IX-	7b	5.12c		E5	27
IX	7c	5.12d			28
IX+	7c+	5.13a	6c		29
X-	8a	5.13b		E6	30
X	8a+	5.13c	7a		31
X+	8b	5.13d		E7	32
XI-	8b+	5.14a	7b		33
XI	8c	5.14b	7c	E8	34
XI+	9a	5.14c			

have even ventured up to 9a, climbing routes that have as yet been too seldom done for their rating to be confirmed.

Climbing as leader and seconding

Sport climbing is done as the leader of a roped party, which means attached by a rope from below, and securing yourself at bolts as you progress. To complete a route means to do it this way. It is not that climbing as second on a top rope is forbidden, but it is seen as second best. Technique and athleticism do of course come into it, but the mental and performance aspects are missing. Completing a route when attached from above does not count, because performance is a combination of various factors, and not just a matter of physical prowess, otherwise climbing would become merely a gymnastic exercise.

Even beginners need to get used to climbing as the leader, starting on very easy routes, which are well within their capabilities, in order to learn not to be afraid of falling and how to cope in situations where this is a distinct possibility. It is by leading climbs that you really learn how to climb; this is the only way to achieve concentration

Left: "seconding."
Above: a pause allows you to study the next sections.

and precision in your movements, practice self-control, and learn how to secure yourself and fall without danger. It is better to tackle a route as leader, attaching yourself to study sections where you do not feel secure, than to climb as second without using resting points, relying on the sense of security that you get from having a rope above you. Climbing second will never allow you to improve your control over the psychological aspect.

POINTS TO REMEMBER

Naturally until you have enough experience you should only tackle routes as leader when closely watched by an instructor or an expert friend. To avoid the risk of unpleasant or dangerous falls, it is essential that you really absorb, until they become almost instinctive reflexes, certain basic rules for progressing along the route and for belaying your partner who is climbing as leader.

Before starting to climb you should make a detailed check on all your equipment, and decide with your partner on how to proceed in the event of any problems.

Before climbing
Climber:
– check that you have fed the harness strap back through and that you are properly tied on.

Belayer:
– check that you have inserted the rope correctly into the security device.

During the climb
Climber:
– the rope should always remain between your body and the rock. If the rope passes behind a leg or a foot, it can cause you to overturn during a fall.

At all times when climbing the rope should remain between your body and the rock (above); if it does not (left) you risk being flipped over backwards if you fall.

82

– you must clip the karabiners correctly. In climbing terminology clipping refers to the action of securing yourself at the safety points found on the wall as you climb. To be more precise, it is the action of attaching the quick-draw to the bolt, and then inserting the rope into the free karabiner. For this to be done correctly the rope should pass through the karabiner from the inside to the outside, namely in such a way that the part of the rope that comes out of the quick-draw is the one that goes to the climber.

If the rope is passed through the quick-draw in the opposite way, if you fall there is a danger that it may fold over against the lever of the karabiner, thus causing it to open and the rope to slip out. A mistake of this sort, which would appear to be obvious, but unfortunately is all too often made by careless climbers, can be the cause of a nasty fall, sometimes with serious consequences if the quick-draw which opens is

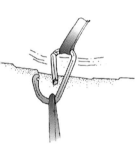

NO: Be careful how you position the quick-draw. If there is any chance of the karabiner opening on a jutting rock, you will need to lengthen the strap.

Clipping is a fundamental maneuver, and it is often not easy, because you are not always comfortably positioned to perform it and it must be done in a totally correct manner.

the one on the first bolt of the route (in this case the climber falls directly to the ground).

Belayer:
– always keep your eyes on your partner.
– position yourself, especially for the first few meters, so that the rope is clear of your partner's legs and not between them, which could impede his movements.
– hold the rope neither too slack nor too tight, and take a step forward in the event of a fall to soften the impact.
– always keep an eye on the end of the rope while lowering your partner, and make a knot at the end of it if you are not sure

whether it is long enough to bring him all the way down to the ground.

Retrieving the quick-draws
If the second person does not retrieve the quick-draws, they will need to be removed during the descent. This is entirely normal, but while it is a very straightforward on a vertical route, if you are descending from an overhang you will need to familiarize yourself with the maneuvers.

The correct way to attach a karabiner to a bolt and to thread the rope through.

In the photo above, the wrong way to clip.

NO: If clipping is not done correctly, the rope could slip out of the karabiner.

TOWARDS THE CLIMBER

TOWARDS THE CLIMBER

You must remember:
– to attach yourself to the rope with a quick-draw before starting the descent, so that it is easy to descend along the rope itself.
– lower yourself down until you reach the level of the quick-draw that needs to be retrieved and pull yourself along the rope until you reach it.
– before detaching the last quick-draw from the bolt and swinging away from the rock like a pendulum, the climber must detach himself from the rope, so as not to drag the belayer with him.
– to watch out for obstacles that may be in the way of your swing. If in doubt, it is better to remain attached to the rope without detaching the quick-draws for the last bit of the descent, and then to climb up again a little way with top rope before letting yourself swing.

During a climb the belayer should always keep a close watch on the climber.

The belayer should hold the rope neither too tight nor too slack, and should stand in such a way that he does not impede the climber during the first few meters.

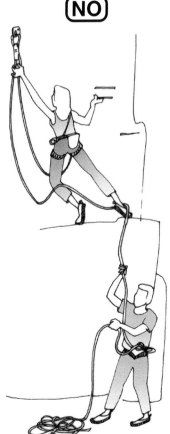

Before beginning the descent you should attach yourself to the rope with a quick-draw, so that you can follow the same line you climbed up and retrieve all your quick-draws from the bolts.

Before detaching the last quick-draw from its bolt and swinging out wide from the rock, check that there are no obstacles that you might collide with as you swing.

Falling

When climbing a route that is at the very limit of your capabilities, a wrong move or exhaustion can cause a fall. In sport climbing a fall is an everyday occurrence. The protective measures that are found on the routes have meant that climbers can forget–deliberately–the fundamental rule of traditional ascents, which is to always climb a route that is one level below your own limit. This has led to an enormous advance in performance in this sport. So you should look on falls as an integral part of climbing on cliffs, not as an exceptional and terrifying event.

However, this does not mean that you should have a reckless attitude towards falling, since every fall is also potentially dangerous. You must learn how to fall, how to control your own reactions during the fall, and also how to evaluate how safe the protective measures really are.

When you feel close to your limit and you know that you have very little control left in your arms, or when you have to tackle a particularly tricky section, you should get the attention of the partner who is belaying you, by shouting out, for example, "look out!" to warn him that you may fall.

What to do when you fall
– keep your hands higher than your harness to avoid being tipped over backwards

– in the case of a very long fall take hold of the rope above the knot in order to keep it in front of you.
– let yourself go without tensing, but with your muscles ready to react, keeping in an almost seated position with your legs in front of you.
– at the end of the fall point your feet towards the rock face with your knees slightly bent so as to absorb the impact.

Below: in cliff climbs falls are considered normal and are not an unusual occurrence.

What not to do in a fall

– do not try to grab the last quick-draw as you fall, because this will break the fall very sharply, and you may injure yourself.

– if you make a controlled fall, i.e. if you let go on purpose, you must not throw yourself outwards with too much of a thrust. Your body tends to fall outwards anyway because of the effects of gravity, and excessive acceleration will only serve to make the final impact with the wall even more violent.

Often you will fall without warning, because a notch in the rock face breaks, or your hand loses its grip, or your foot slips off a precarious foothold. In this situation you react instinctively, and so it is really important to have thoroughly learnt the correct way to react, so that it becomes automatic in the event of a fall.

Bolts

It is equally important to be able to spot situations that present real danger, i.e. when it is better not to fall, because the bolts are dangerous:

– bolts that are not reliable because they are old and in a bad state; best not to risk jumping, especially if they are positioned far apart.

– badly positioned bolts; if you fall there is a risk of falling on a ledge and breaking your ankles, or hitting a projecting rock or rock spike, with consequences that may easily be imagined.

A well bolted route does not necessarily mean one on which the bolts are very close together, but one where the belays are placed in logical positions for attaching karabiners, and in such a way as to guarantee a safe fall.

In such situations experienced climbers are able to judge whether they are capable of tackling the problems on the route without risking a fall, but it is better, where possible, to avoid such situations altogether.

If you are unsure of your own ability or, worse, if you realize that you are unable to

If you let go with your hands, raise them above your head immediately to avoid being tipped over backwards.

NO

ROPE TOO TIGHT –
STATIC FALL

region. The rope should only be pulled tight in order to avoid the climber colliding with a rock spike or reaching the ground.

As a general rule it is better to leave the rope a little slack and to step forward if your partner falls so as to soften the fall, i.e. what is known technically as dynamic belaying. Obviously there is a happy medium in everything. You should not just hand out a lot of rope any old how, but give out the right amount to suit the type of wall.

YES

ROPE SLIGHTLY SLACK –
DYNAMIC FALL

make it, it is much better to abandon a karabiner on the rock face and to let yourself be lowered down. (It is a good rule to always keep some old ones that you can sacrifice in emergency situations.)

Lastly, you should not forget that when falling, as at every other moment in climbing, there are two protagonists, and the actions of the belayer are just as important as those of the climber. It often happens that the belayer gathers up all the rope so as to lessen the length of the fall. This, however, means that the fall is all the more violent and a static finish causes a very sharp counter blow on the lumbar

Completing a route

Contrary to other sporting activities, climbing is a sport in which, whatever the level, performance matters. Every route that is completed, in which you have invested physical and mental energy by climbing close to your personal limitations, represents a very satisfying performance. It is important to emphasize once again exactly what completion means: a climber can say that he has completed a route when he has free-climbed it, i.e. as the leader, without resting at a belay, falling or using any artificial means, which means using only his own strength in a "pure" way.

A distinction can normally be made between three types of completion:

• <u>On sight flash</u>: without having ever tried or studied it first, and without having ever watched anyone else attempting it. This is the most difficult.

• <u>Beta flash</u>: at the first attempt, after having first watched another climber going up, or climbing with instructions from a partner who already knows it.

• <u>Redpoint</u>: after having attempted it several times previously, i.e. after having worked at the most difficult sections, finally succeeding in overcoming them and then putting them all together.

Climbing on sight is the most demanding, requiring an excellent and instantaneous ability to "read" a section, since an incorrect decision as to the right movement or sequence of movements to make can often not be rectified, leading inevitably to a fall, and thus to a failed attempt at the route.

Generally, in the redpoint method it is possible to complete more difficult routes than can be done on sight, since over the course of various attempts you eventually memorize certain sections, and how to climb them in the most economical and effective manner, until you can climb the whole route without rests or pauses.

Completing a route, has a very positive effect; it allows you to gain a greater sense of security in your own equipment and a better awareness of your own potential. Climbing on sight is psychologically most rewarding, as it presents the challenge of tackling an unknown section, and it is also a way of improving your tactics.

Above: sport climbing is always a test of ability, strength, technique, and concentration.

On the other hand, redpointing a route allows you to memorize movements and to climb at your very best; besides this, trying a section until you finally succeed in overcoming it is excellent training, which raises the level of your technique.

Single pitch and multi-pitch routes
Sport climbing is limited to single pitch routes (of a single rope length).

However, multi-pitch routes also exist, (see 2, Materials and Equipment) sometimes several hundred feet in length, fitted out in accordance with sport climbing criteria. While multi-pitch routes do not require mountaineering experience, there is an underlying assumption that anyone who tackles them is extremely familiar with all safety maneuvers.

Besides, even if the routes are fitted out with expanding or screw-in bolts, these are placed further apart than they are on single

Top left: climbing "on sight," without ever having tried or studied the route.
Top right: a "worked" route is one that you complete after having made several attempts at it.
Above: in "flash" climbing, you try to complete a route at your first attempt after having first watched others climbing it.

pitch routes; in other words they are much tougher climbs. Bolts are always located so as to avoid climbers coming to any harm, but you need to allow for the possibility of long falls, if you are not up to the route. In the guidebooks you will generally find the lowest level that you are required to have mastered for the route, i.e. the level of difficulty at which you must be able to move easily. For example, you may find written next to the name of the route: "7a max – 6b obligatory." This means that the most difficult sections of the route are up to level 7a in difficulty, with the safety points positioned in such a way that the difficulty between one bolt and another is never greater than level 6b.

On the sections that are 6b or easier the safety points will be quite far apart, which means that it is important to have total mastery of the level required and be used to climbing without getting worried even when quite far away from a bolt.

When you attempt a long route, choose a partner you trust. Make sure you know how good the bolts on the route are, so as not to end up with a nasty surprise when you are halfway up, or at a point where it is no longer possible to turn back. Climbing in a natural environment, with a void below you, is a priceless experience, which creates a relationship between the climber and the rock face, and makes him feel one with nature. But it is an experience towards which you must build up gradually, starting with routes that are well below the level you have reached, so that you gain confidence on this new playing field.

Alternating multi-pitch routes with days climbing on low cliffs is excellent mental training for overcoming fear and building up confidence in yourself. You will also discover a new and different dimension to climbing.

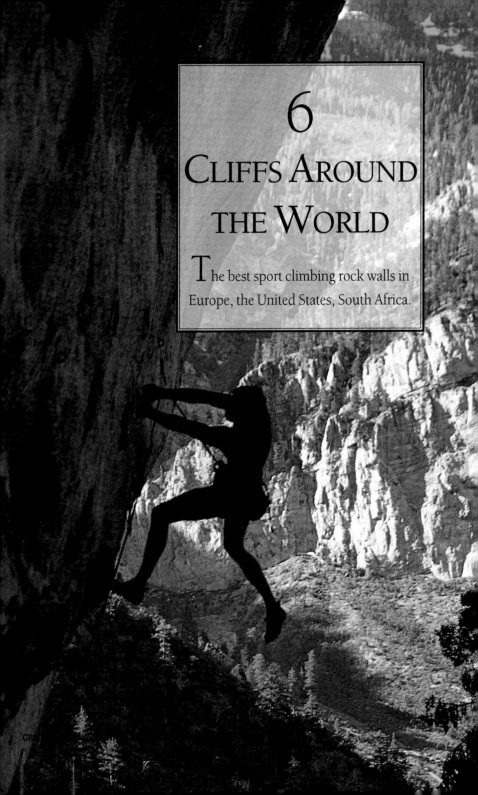

6
CLIFFS AROUND THE WORLD

The best sport climbing rock walls in Europe, the United States, South Africa.

ARCO DI TRENTO

How to get there: take the exit for Rovereto Sud off the Modena-Brennero autostrada. From here follow signs for Mori and then for Arco.

Rock type: very variable limestone, with notches, pipes, and holes.

Routes: from 20–500m (66 to 1640 ft.), fitted with expanding and screw-in bolts.

Difficulty level: from easy to extreme.

Season: all year round.

Further details: being so close to Lake Garda means that Arco has an extremely favorable micro-climate, mild and pleasant all year round. There are many cliffs, for every style and level of climbing. A guidebook is essential.

FINALE LIGURE
How to get there: take the exit for Finale Ligure off the Modena-Brennero autostrada.
Rock type: pitted limestone.
Routes: from 10–200m (33 to 656 ft.), fitted with ex-panding and screw-in bolts.
Difficulty level: from easy to extreme.
Season: all year round.
Further details: numerous different climbing areas. A guidebook is essential.

FERENTILLO
How to get there: from Terni (Perugia) take the SS 209 for Val Nerina until you get to the group of houses at Ferentillo.
Rock type: mostly limestone with pockets and pipes.
Routes: from 10–80m (33 to 262 ft.), fitted with expanding and screw-in bolts.
Difficulty level: from easy to extreme.
Season: from autumn to spring.
Further details: numerous climbing areas close to each other, deep in the glorious Umbrian hills. A guidebook is useful.

GROTTI
How to get there: from Rieti follow the SS 578 in the direction of Avezzano. It is not far from Ferentillo.
Rock type: compact pitted conglomerate.
Routes: from 12–35m (39 to 115 ft.), excellently fitted with bolts.
Difficulty level: from difficult to extreme.
Season: from autumn to spring.
Further details: a very beautiful cliff, but fairly specialized.

CALA GONONE

How to get there: from Olbia take the SS 125 south as far as Dorgali (Nuoro), then take a left fork for Cala Gonone.

ISILI

How to get there: from Cagliari take the SS 131 for Oristano as far as Monastir. From here take the SS 128 for Isilli.

Rock type: very worn limestone.

Routes: fitted with expanding bolts, from 12–120m (39 to 394 ft.).

Difficulty level: from easy to difficult at Cala Gonone, from easy to extreme at Isili.

Season: from autumn to spring.

Further details: impressive rock, unique setting. Sardinia's potential is still far from being exhausted. You will need a guidebook to find the various sectors.

PALERMO

There are two areas to which it is worth drawing attention: Monte Pellegrino-Bauso Rosso and Rocca di Cefalù.

MONTE PELLEGRINO-BAUSO ROSSO

How to get there: to reach the Monte Pellegrino and Bauso Rosso sections, you go into the Parco della Favorita, across the Piazza dei Leoni (Palermo). From here you follow the road for Mondello.

ROCCA DI CEFALÙ

How to get there: from Palermo take either the autostrada or the coastal road as far as Cefalù. As you leave the citadel, heading for Messina, you turn up a narrow road that leads to steps that take you to the Rocca (signposted).
Rock type: pink and gray limestone.
Routes: from 10–150m (33 to 492 ft.), fitted with bolts.
Difficulty level: from easy to difficult.
Season: from autumn to spring.
Further details: beautiful climbing cliffs, whose potential is as yet relatively undiscovered, with a large number of medium-easy routes.

CEÜSE

How to get there: from Gap follow signs for Veynes, by the D994, until you reach the resort of Freissinouse, where you turn off onto the D19, sign-posted Sigoyer. As you leave the town take the road for Col des Guerins.

Rock type: compacted lime-stone with pockets and pipes on the overhangs and small holes and fissures on the slabs.

Routes: from 30–120m (98 to 394 ft.), fitted with expand-ing and screw-in bolts.

Difficulty level: from easy to extreme.

Season: late spring, summer and autumn.

Further details: nearly four and a half miles (7km) of perfect limestone in the heart of the Hautes Alpes. Ceüse is the biggest cliff (and perhaps also the most beautiful) in the world (the only one that can be seen by satellite).

VERDON

How to get there: from Nice take the N85 to Castellane. As you leave the town follow the D952 as far as La Palud sur Verdon.

Rock type: limestone with pockets, and vertical and horizontal fissures.

Routes: from 20–350m (66 to 1148 ft.), routes mainly fitted with bolts, but also a good number of traditional routes, requiring protection.

Difficulty level: from easy to extreme.

Season: from spring to autumn.

Further details: the Verdon gorge is one of the places which witnessed the birth of sport climbing. It is essential to get hold of a guidebook and to choose your route very carefully, as there are both sport climbing and traditional routes.

BUOUX
How to get there: from Aix en Provence follow the N7 for 6.2 miles (10km) and then take the detour for Rognes, along the N543. From Rognes take the D943 towards Apt, and just after Lourmarin turn off onto the D113.
Rock type: pitted limestone.
Routes: from 10–130m (33 to 426 ft.), fitted with bolts.
Difficulty level: from easy to extreme.
Season: all year round, but best in spring and autumn.
Further details: an historic cliff, discovered at the end of the fifties. During the eighties many of the first difficult routes in Europe were climbed here. On private land, access is strictly controlled and only certain sections are authorized. A guidebook of the area is essential.

CIMAI
How to get there: from Toulon take the N8 as far as the village of St. Anne D'Evenos. From here turn right onto the D62 which brings you in 1.9 miles (3km) to the parking place under the cliff.
Rock type: limestone.
Routes: from 10–60m (33 to 197 ft.), excellently fitted out.
Difficulty level: from easy to extreme.
Season: from autumn to spring.
Further details: Cimai can boast some of the first really challenging routes in Europe. Having rather fallen from popularity in recent years, it is a beautiful cliff to rediscover.

CALANQUES

How to get there: From Marseilles take the coastal road towards La Corniche. Then turn left for Bonneveine (for access to the Gardiole, Luminy, Morgiou, and Sourmiou sectors), or carry straight on in the direction of La Plage (for access to the Marseilleveyre and Les Goudes sectors).

Rock type: pitted limestone, with notches and pipes.

Routes: from 20–150m (66 to 492 ft.), fitted with expanding and screw-in bolts.

Difficulty level: from easy to extreme.

Season: from autumn to spring.

Further details: extremely beautiful setting, and numerous cliffs that are often difficult to find. A guidebook is essential.

FRANKENJURA
How to get there: an area of the Black Forest to the north west of Nuremberg.
Rock type: limestone.
Routes: from 10–25m (33 to 82 ft.), fitted with bolts.
Difficulty level: from easy to extreme.
Season: spring and autumn.
Further details: an area with many low cliffs of a monolithic type, scattered around the forest. It is essential to have a guidebook to find your way around, also because access is forbidden to many areas at certain times of the year, when birds are nesting.

SIURANA

How to get there: from Tarragona take the superstrada to Reus. Then follow the 420 for Falset, and then to Les Borges del Camp, from where you head for Cornudella.

Rock type: limestone.

Routes: from 15–100m (49 to 328 ft.), fitted with expanding and screw-in bolts.

Difficulty level: from easy to extreme.

Season: from autumn to spring.

Further details: the various climbing areas are spread out around the atmospheric village of Siurana, the last Saracen outpost in Spain to surrender to the Christian armies. The remains of a mediaeval fortress, which looked out from the rock over a vast region, can still be seen.

EL CHORRO

How to get there: from Malaga take the road for Antequera, and then follow signs for the Valle de Abdalajis. This takes you to El Chorro.
It is also the only climbing location that can be reached by rail, with the train stopping in the village of El Chorro itself.
Rock type: limestone.
Routes: from 10–200m (33 to 660 ft.). Not always very well equipped.
Difficulty level: from easy to extreme.
Season: from autumn to spring.
Further details: a beautiful wild location, but sites rather too scattered. There are numerous sectors, many of which are a little difficult to reach. It is essential that you get hold of a guidebook.

CUENCA

How to get there: located halfway between Valencia and Madrid. The climbing areas can be found beside the road leading to Tragacete.

Rock type: limestone with pockets and notches on most of the routes, and a few with pipes.

Routes: from 15–100m (49 to 330 ft.), excellently fitted with expanding and screw-in bolts.

Difficulty level: from easy to extreme.

Season: Ideal in spring and autumn; a little cold in winter.

Further details: a very peaceful and little used place. Many extremely beautiful areas. Compared to the amazing quantity of rocky cliffs that surround the city, there are very few prepared routes. It is still being developed, and is potentially one of the biggest climbing locations in the world.

MALHAM COVE
How to get there: from Leeds follow signs for Malham.
Rock type: limestone, mostly with notches, often sheer.
Routes: from 10–30m (33 to 99 ft.), fitted out with bolts, or requiring protection with traditional methods.
Difficulty level: from easy to extreme. The majority of the easy routes are VS (traditional style climbing). The good bolted routes start from level 6c+. Below this level easy routes fitted out with bolts are poor.
Season: climbing all year round, but in winter you need sun and a north wind. The central section of the wall remains dry even if it rains.
Further details: a rock amphitheater almost 330 feet (100m) high. Most routes are fitted with bolts, but at the sides there are also traditional routes. It is located within the beautiful Yorkshire Dales National Park.

SMITH ROCKS
How to get there: 10 minutes north of city of Bend (Oregon), on highway 41.
Rock type: volcanic.
Routes: from 25–50m (82 to 164 ft.), with bolts.
Difficulty level: from easy to extreme.
Season: spring and autumn, possible in winter, very hot in summer.
Further details: historic cliff where some of the first really demanding climbs of the continent were completed. It is a spectacular place, both because of its setting and quality of its routes, most of which are at a great height.

YOSEMITE
How to get there: situated north of the Sierra Nevada Mountains (California), two hours' drive north of Fresno on highway 41.
Rock type: granite.
Routes: from 25–1000m (82 to 3300 ft.); traditional, artificial and modern routes, protected with friends, nuts and bolts.
Difficulty level: from easy to extreme.
Season: from spring to autumn.
Further details: Yosemite is one of the most historical climbing locations in the world. It offers an enormous number of routes, on excellent rock, that are always very demanding. Climbing is mostly traditional. There are only a few routes that are completely fitted out with bolts, mostly located in the Tuolomne Meadows area, towards the Tioga Pass.

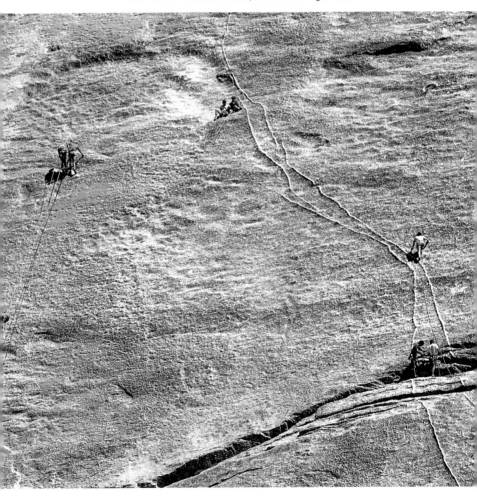

RED ROCKS
How to get there: 45 minutes west of Las Vegas (Nevada), along the Charleston Road.
Rock type: compact sandstone.
Routes: single pitch and multi-pitch routes, some modern with bolts and some traditional, requiring protection.
Difficulty level: from easy to extreme.
Season: from autumn to spring.
Further details: stupendous routes over unusual red rock, in the middle of the desert, close to the gambling capital. All sectors are close to one another, but it is impossible to find them without the guidebook.

MT. CHARLESTON

How to get there: 45 minutes west of Las Vegas (Nevada), along highway 156 and then turning off onto highway 157.

Rock type: very compact white limestone, with pockets.

Routes: from 20–35m (66 to 115 ft.), fitted out with bolts.

Difficulty level: from difficult to extreme.

Season: from spring to autumn.

Further details: At at altitude of nearly 9900 ft. (3000m), ideal for summer climbing. The rock here has been described as the most beautiful limestone in the USA. But: the few routes there are mostly very difficult.

CITY OF ROCKS

How to get there: two and a half hours north of Salt Lake City (Utah), along highways 15 and 84 until you reach the city of Malta. From here, by following signs for Almo, you reach the City of Rocks Natural Reserve (Idaho).

Rock type: granite.

Routes: from 10–50m (33 to 165 ft.), with bolts.

Difficulty level: from easy to extreme.

Season: from the end of spring until autumn.

Further details: unique setting, beautiful rock, and excellent routes for climbers of all levels.

NATAL
How to get there: from Durban take N3 towards Pietermaritzburg then take Shongweni Reserve exit.
Rock type: granite.
Routes: from 10–200m (33 to 660 ft.). Modern with bolts, and traditional.
Difficulty level: from easy to difficult.
Season: April to October.
Further details: superb location but not easy to find. Guidebook essential. Protection necessary on long routes.

CEDERBERG

How to get there: nature reserve three hours north of Cape Town. Reached from the town of Clanwilliam.

Rock type: granite.

Routes: from 10–250m (33 to 820 ft.), modern routes with bolts, and traditional routes needing protection.

Difficulty level: from easy to difficult.

Season: from November to April.

Further details: License to enter Cederberg nature reserve from the Cape Nature Conservation Office at Citrusdal, or Algeria.

7

BOULDERING

Origins and spirit of bouldering.
Equipment and techniques. Completing a
boulder. Evaluation of difficulty ratings.

CRISTIAN BRENNA / ERMENEGILDA, 7b+ / MESCHIA (ITALY)

INTRODUCTION

Bouldering is a somewhat unusual side of sport climbing. Although it has been going on for a very long time, it is only very recently that it has been recognized as an area of competition on an equal footing with difficulty trials. (This is how the classical branch of sport climbing, with a rope, is defined in the competition context; see 9, Competitions). It was in 1999 that the first Bouldering World Cup took place, with a wide-reaching competition circuit.

If it is compared with climbing on cliffs, with which this book has been so far concerned, a number of major differences can be seen:
– no rope is used in bouldering.
– the boulders, also known as "problems," are a very short sequence of movements, at most 10 to 12. It is also possible to attempt longer routes on the blocks, such as traverses of 30 to 40 movements, but these are in fact called traverses and not boulders, even though they are part of this sport.

– bouldering does not need a ready equipped wall; every stone mass is potentially a bouldering site, and all that you need to do is clean off any moss, lichen and soil, and find lines of hand or footholds on which you can attempt a series of movements. This does of course mean that in a bouldering area it is much more difficult, compared to cliffs, to find and recognize the boulders, unless you are accompanied by someone familiar with the area who can point them out. Guidebooks do exist for the best known sites, but they are not always sufficient, and without the help of a climber from the area you are likely to waste a lot of time wandering from one boulder to another in search of one to attempt.

Below: bouldering is in fact a sequence of climbing movements on rock masses and artificial structures.

– The aim of bouldering is to successfully get to the end of a section and, obviously, to cope with increasingly difficult challenges. A little bit like climbing cliff routes, but with one major difference: a cliff route usually requires great stamina and continuity, while bouldering is an exercise in pure strength, and is a matter of a few seconds and a few movements that use every shred of energy that you have. It is not of course simply a demonstration of strength; you also need a good technique, combined with speed and co-ordination, in order to resolve sections that seem impossible at first sight.

WHAT IS BOULDERING?

It comes from boulder, which simply means a massive rock; the English term has been universally adopted, and is used in a broader sense to mean a short sequence of movements.

So bouldering is climbing without ropes on large rocks, or on artificial structures, on routes which should not, for your personal safety, be more than 4–5m (13 to 16 feet) off the ground (though in a natural environment they may also be higher) and which in competitions are reduced to 3–4m (10 to 13 feet). A key feature of this sport is the limited number of movements of which a boulder may consist if it is to qualify for that name.

Below: every large rock is a potential bouldering site, where all your energy reserves are used up in a matter of seconds.

THE ORIGINS OF BOULDE-RING

In the last five or six years the bouldering craze has really taken off, attracting an enormous following among the very young, but also among the diehards of cliff climbing. It is, however, a mistake to see it as a new sport; it is more correct to call it a rediscovery, as the precursors of modern bouldering can actually be traced back to the end of the 19th century.

The Bleausards

The first traces of bouldering can be found on the great rocks that lie scattered around the beautiful forest of Fontainebleau, on the outskirts of Paris. As early as the end of the 19th century some mountaineers are known to have trained here so as to be able to deal with rocky sections in their Alpine endeavors, finding in the various faces of these rocks an example of every type of movement and climb that may be encountered on a rock face in the mountains.

By the start of the 20th century being a Bleau habitué had already developed certain connotations, indicating belonging to a group, and in 1924 Le Groupe de Bleau (G.D.B.) officially came into being, hence the name Bleausards. One of the

The forest of Fontainebleau (France) was already a training ground for climbing at the end of the 19th century. The photograph shows the block known as the Elephant.

many conditions of belonging to this group was to have camped at least ten times ... in the forest of Fontainebleau.

During the Second World War Fontainebleau became the Parisians' mountain. Prevented from reaching the high Alpine peaks by forces beyond their control, heedless of the curfew, they continued to camp in the forest and to experiment with novel situations and problems on the rocks. This was the start of really difficult challenges and the first boulder circuits.

After the war bouldering became very popular and little by little, from being merely a training ground, boulders became an aim in themselves, with their own rules and their own difficulty scale.

On the Fontainebleau rocks, bouldering has never gone out of fashion, and the reputation of the Parisian stone and the most famous boulders in the world are today magnets for both Bleausards and international climbers.

The Camp Four blocks

Precursors can also be found in America. In the fifties, when the immense Yosemite cliffs were first "conquered" and at the time when a new vision of climbing was being formed that would spread to Europe, climbers were spending a lot of time in Camp Four, between one climb and the next. This famous campsite in the Yosemite park, located under the vast walls of El Capitan and the Half Dome still evokes the memory of a golden age of climbing for climbers from all over the world. Around the camp lie huge and beautiful rocks, on which very demanding climbs have been pioneered over the years. The first people to start the sport of bouldering were the leading climbers of the "great" days, such as Royal Robbins, Tom Frost, Yvon Chuinard, John Gill (nicknamed "the human fly" because of his extraordinary skill in climbing any rock whatsoever), and others. The difference between the Bleausards and these Americans is that the latter practiced bouldering not only as training for the big walls, but also and above all for pleasure, as a trial of their skills, as a game in its own right.

Left: John Gill, one of the precursors of modern bouldering (from Royal Robbins by Pat Ament).

The emergence of bouldering as a sport

Parisians and Californians may be the most famous ancestors of bouldering, but they are not the only ones to have discovered climbing on large rocks. From the sixties onwards, all over the place, climbers began to spend time on rock masses, using them primarily as a training ground where they could improve their fitness and technique in preparation for big climbs in the mountains. But bouldering was still not perceived as an activity in its own right (as it was beginning to be, for example, in Fontainebleau), or rather there were very few people who climbed the blocks for their own enjoyment, always trying to find more difficult routes.

Attitudes changed with the advent of low artificial structures for training, "homemade" rock walls or walls set up in a gym, with wooden and resin foot and handholds variously angled, and mattresses at the base to soften falls.

Climbers began to use these walls to work on specific skills, alternating circuits of stamina with short sequences of power movements (bouldering in fact), even improvising competitions between friends. This led to the rediscovery of known rock masses, and the search for new ones where possible lines could be discovered from scratch. On rocks the rules of the game are different from those on artificial walls; there are no mattresses at the base, and the risk of being injured in a fall is high. So it requires greater courage, maximum concentration, and one or more companions to catch the climber in the event of a fall.

In the next paragraphs will be found a description of the equipment necessary to get started on bouldering and tips on how to "spot" correctly.

Left: low indoor structures are ideal for specific training.
Above: it is best to tackle a boulder with the help of a friend, because there is always a risk of falling.

EQUIPMENT

Bouldering does not require a large amount of equipment; neither ropes nor harnesses, quick-draws nor descenders are used. What you do need are climbing shoes, preferably quick to put on and take off (either ballerina style or with Velcro fastenings) because they are used for the attempt on the boulder and then taken off straightaway.

Crash Pad

A brilliant invention of the last decade, the crash pad is a type of portable mattress that folds up into two or three sections depending on the model, and can be carried over your shoulder like a rucksack. When it is open it covers a surface of about 3m² (ten square feet) and is about 10cm (four inches) thick. The material inside is

The crash pad used to soften falls is a folding mattress that can easily be carried on your shoulder.

fairly stiff and does not flatten much under impact, thus successfully softening the blow, and it is covered in a particularly resilient material that is resistant to tears and abrasions.

Magnesite and magnesite bag

Magnesite is totally indispensable. The bag is tied to your waist by a cord or left on the ground (there is almost never time to apply magnesite to your hands while engaged on a block). Before every attempt you apply it abundantly, so that you use much more of it than you would on cliffs. This is why the maxi magnesite bag came into being, designed specifically for bouldering. Large and spacious, it is always left on the ground, at the base of the rock being tackled.

Small brush

There are people who even carry a brush on cliffs, to clean off excessive magnesite prints while they are climbing a route. In bouldering it is an essential item, because on a very difficult section a hold that is slippery because of too much magnesite or a little bit of soil could easily hinder performance. There are also wire and bristle brushes that are essential for cleaning moss and lichen off a new boulder.

SAFETY

With or without crash pad, every fall in bouldering is a fall to the ground. So efforts must be made to avoid injuries such as bruised heels, sprained ankles, and back problems, by following some basic rules.

Tackling a boulder

1. Remove from the base of the boulder any obstacle that can be moved, such as branches and stones.

2. Do not just ask anybody who happens to be there to catch you, but a partner who is prepared, and with whom you have an excellent understanding. Catching is far from easy and it entails huge responsibility. The spotter (this is the correct terminology for the catcher) has a very important task: to make sure you reach the ground without injury. If you are to concentrate solely on your movements and on your performance, you must have a mind that is completely free from fear and hesitation, and for this you need to be able to trust your spotter completely.

Before attempting a boulder, you should clear the ground of all obstacles.

3. The crash pad is positioned under the most problematic section, at the point where you are likely to land.

4 When you fall, do not rely entirely on your spotter, but try to land on your legs; this means reacting very quickly, with your muscles primed, ready to absorb the impact of the ground with your legs.

"Spotting" for a partner
The three priorities are:
– Protect the climber's head and back
– Direct your partner's fall so that they land well.
– Lessen the force of the fall and lighten the impact on the ground or on the crash pad.

Above and right: although only a short distance, every fall can cause serious injuries, and so it is best to have one or more trustworthy companions to catch you and to position the crash pad under the most difficult sections.

To be able to catch successfully, it is useful to know the sequence of the problem being tackled and to anticipate your partner's moves. For this it is a wise idea to get your partner to explain the boulder to you (especially if you are not already acquainted with it) and above all to know which is the trickiest bit, which may easily cause a fall.

While the climber is engaged on the boulder, you must focus your attention on their center of gravity, which in women is at waist height and in men a few centimeters higher. You must not make the mistake of being distracted by the movements of hands, arms, feet, or legs. All of these parts of the body can distance themselves from the rock giving the impression that the climber is falling, while in fact they may be making excellent progress.

In certain situations it may be that there are immovable obstacles near the rock (large stones or a tree). In such a situation it is better to stand on or near the obstacle and thrust your partner firmly away from it.

If a fall should occur in the first few movements the climber will land unharmed on the crash pad; if the fall occurs at a dangerous section the spotter should push the climber forwards towards a safe landing.

When the climber is in a position where they may fall straight down, you should stand as close as possible to them and take hold of them by the hips, accompanying their fall and lessening the impact. The climber will absorb the rest with their legs.

If the climber falls from the top of an overhang they cannot be caught safely by a spotter who stays underneath the boulder. They could easily strike their back on the rock behind. It is therefore better to stand guard on that rock.

When the climber is on an overhanging rock they could easily fall on their back. In such a situation you should catch them by getting hold of them at the armpits. You should push their torso forwards to straighten them up as they fall, and then try to accompany them to the ground.

The bouldering spirit

If practiced with due care, bouldering is a fun and stimulating sport, accessible to everyone.

It is the most athletic and also the most light-hearted aspect of climbing. In some people's view, it is also the most sensual, in the sense of "linked to the senses." Successfully resolving a difficult section does in fact depend very much on being in complete harmony with your own body, and on feeling movements within yourself.

The absence of harness, rope and quick-draws gives a great sense of liberation, and attempts on individual problems often last barely more than a few seconds, in which you need to release all the energy at your

In bouldering it is essential to have good balance and physical strength.

disposal, or hold your breath to get over a section where your balance is pushed to its limit. Reaching the top of a boulder after a series of movements that have used every fiber in your body, is a very powerful and liberating feeling, and gives a real adrenaline rush. Lastly, bouldering is of course also a trial ground for experimenting on all the possible climbing techniques, and from this point of view it would benefit everyone to have a go at it, as an alternative to other types of climbing.

Psychologically it is less demanding than climbing cliffs, since, besides being over in a very short time, the climber is not constrained to overcome each boulder at all costs. After a few vain attempts you can calmly decide to try another. On a cliff route, on the other hand, you still need to

Every problem is different; it may require great strength or great delicacy.

reach the rest point in order to retrieve the materials.

Bouldering is also the most sociable form of climbing. In other branches of climbing the relationship between the climber and the wall is of primary importance. When you are engaged on a cliff route and concentrating hard, the world around you ceases to exist, and this state can last for the duration of the attempt, or at least until you fall. This aspect of climbing is considerably reduced in bouldering: when attempting a boulder you also need total concentration, but it does not last more than a minute. You can try difficult sections again and again without boring the partner who is securing you at the base of the route. Climbing sessions with friends can be relaxed or competitive in the extreme, but there are also always moments of companionship and closeness. Besides this, when attempting blocks that are at the very limit of your ability, it is much more important than it is in cliff climbing to be with other climbers of the same level. You can then measure yourself against them on the same boulders, and obtain through healthy competition the necessary motivation to really give it your all.

This does not mean that bouldering is better than climbing on cliffs or on long routes, just that they are different sports. It could perhaps be said that the latter two, because of their

In some cases getting over difficult sections depends on understanding what the right movements are, found by trial and error during attempts.

psychological aspect and the extremely individual relationship that the climber has with the route, have a greater fascination and completeness, while bouldering is more sociable and, from a performance point of view, represents the very essence of movement. It is an exercise in power and technique completely independent of other factors.

Of course, anyone who prefers complete peace can also do bouldering alone. In this case, however, even if you are armed with a crash pad, it is not wise to attempt very demanding movements if a fall would be very dangerous.

Left: no other single sport is as sociable as bouldering. Below: if you are alone you should not risk potentially dangerous sections.

Boulder classification

Bouldering too has its difficulty scale, which appears very similar to that used in sport climbing, but in practice is very different.

The major difference is this:
– On a cliff route the difficulty rating is determined by the most difficult sections and by the continuity needed to coordinate all your movements.
– On a boulder the rating is determined by a single section, and the difficulty, being so short, is thus extremely concentrated.

In Europe the French scale is used, which has a range of 2 to 8b+, and this can give rise to misunderstanding in those who are not well acquainted with bouldering. In fact, it is not possible to compare a boulder rating with a cliff rating. To give an example, it may be said that a single boulder section rated at 5+ could be more difficult than a 20m (66 feet) long cliff route rated at 6b, which totals 35 movements. It is the stringing together of the whole route that gives it the overall rating of 6b. On the other hand single sections that are 6b in difficulty may be found on routes with an overall rating of 7a. No one has yet managed a boulder rated higher

than 8b+; the problems encountered at this level are extreme, and there may well be nothing to match them on cliff routes that have a rating of 9a.

So a climber who is capable of 8b on cliffs may be unable to move at all on a boulder rated 7b. Conversely someone who has only been concentrating on strength, and who manages in a few attempts to resolve 8b boulder problems, may not have the continuity necessary to successfully climb a 7b route on a cliff.

In America, to avoid any misunderstanding, a difficulty scale just for boulders has been introduced, which goes from V0 to V14, and in which V0 includes levels as far as 6a on the French scale and V14 corresponds to the French 8b+.

Completion

Successfully completing a challenge is known as closing the boulder.

After you have cleaned the boulder, you can plot out lines of hand and footholds, and begin to try out various movements, until you are able to link together a sequence, which allows you to solve the problem. The end of a boulder may be the

Determining the difficulty rating of a boulder cannot be compared to ratings on cliff routes; it is determined by a single section, in which difficulty and effort are concentrated.

top of the mass or simply a very good hold, on which both your hands fit. The pioneer of the boulder (i.e. the one who first manages to complete it), may spend a long time trying out the right body position, clever foot movements and various other maneuvers before being able to resolve the problem. This is especially true of extremely tough boulders, but sometimes even intermediate level blocks, where movements are not instinctive, and require great delicacy and technique, can take many efforts before being solved. Often only one effective method exists to resolve a particular section, and every other movement is purely a waste of energy.

Successfully completing a boulder at the first attempt, as a flash, i.e. after having

studied it carefully or had it explained by someone else, represents the best possible performance; it is as good as climbing on sight in cliff climbing. Completing a boulder on sight is not possible. Climbing a cliff on sight precludes the possibility of touching the holds before attempting the route. When, however, a boulder is being studied for the first time, even if nobody points out the necessary movements, there is always the possibility of testing out the hand and footholds, often even the highest ones, by climbing to the top of the block by the easiest route.

Completing a boulder nearly always means getting to the top of the rock mass (above), but the end can also be a very good handhold where you can fit both your hands (left).

8
BOULDERING
LOCATIONS

The most famous boulders in Europe, the United States, and South Africa.

VAL DI MELLO
How to get there: from the Valtellina valley, follow the Masino valley until you reach San Martino.
Rock type: granite.
Difficulty level: from easy to difficult.
Season: from spring to autumn.
Further details: the boulders are located in the Sasso Remeno area, in Val Massino and in Val di Mello. It is a fantastic setting, with many blocks still unsolved. In Val di Mello it is also possible to do traditional climbing on beautiful long routes, requiring protection.

MESCHIA

How to get there: from Ascoli Piceno follow the strada statale for Rome, then follow signs for Rocca Fluvione, Montegallo, and Meschia.

Rock type: sandstone.

Difficulty level: from easy to difficult.

Season: all year round.

Further details: location known only to a few, with enormous potential. Many boulders are still unclimbed. The chestnut woods where the blocks are found are private property.

CRESCIANO
How to get there: from Bellinzona Nord follow the road for Biasca until you reach Cresciano, take the small turning on the right and follow it to the end.
Rock type: granite.
Difficulty level: from easy to extreme.
Season: from late autumn to the start of spring.
Further details: one of the top bouldering sites in Europe. The boulders are found in woods that are private property. Be careful where you park.

FONTAINEBLEAU
How to get there: from Paris take the autoroute for Lyon and take the exit for Fontainebleau.
Rock type: sandstone.
Difficulty level: from easy to extreme.
Season: from autumn to spring.
Further details: a historic bouldering site; the famous forest now boasts dozens of different areas and thousands of boulders. It is impossible to find your way around the maze of rocks without a guide or someone who knows the area.

THE ROACHES
How to get there: Reached from the town of Buxton, following the road for Leek (south).
Rock type: same as at Stanage.
Difficulty level: from easy to extreme.
Season: all year round, spring and autumn being the best periods; more sheltered from the winds than Stanage.
Further details: besides the boulders there are also traditional routes needing protection, from 10–40m (33 to 135 ft.) high, the majority of which are medium-easy but without bolts.

PEAK DISTRICT

How to get there: from Manchester to Hathersage, in the Peak District National Park. There are two sites here: Stanage Edge and The Roaches.

STANAGE EDGE

How to get there: Reached by a steep uphill road (Ringinglow Road) from Hathersage.

Rock type: very rough sandstone, with rounded holds; it dries very quickly and offers amazing grip.

Difficulty level: from easy to extreme.

Season: all year round, but better to avoid very windy days. Spring and autumn are the best periods.

Further details: historic site for traditional climbing since the 1900s. More than 1000 routes on a cliff of about 4 miles (7km) in length, but not even a single bolt!

HUECO TANKS

How to get there: a National Park, located 30 minutes east of El Paso (Texas), along highway 62/180.

Rock type: granite.

Difficulty level: from easy to extreme.

Season: from late autumn to the start of spring.

Further details: definitely one of the best bouldering sites in the world. Many areas are prohibited or only accessible with a ranger. Information can be obtained about this on the spot.

JOSHUA TREE

How to get there: nature park two and a half hours east of Los Angeles (California), along highways 10 and 62 north.

Rock type: granite.

Difficulty level: from easy to extreme.

Season: from autumn to spring.

Further details: excellent location in the middle of the desert, famous for its characteristic trees and rounded boulders scattered all over the place. There are also climbing routes requiring protection.

BISHOP - BUTTERMILK
How to get there: from Los Angeles take highway 14 and then highway 395 heading north, until you reach the town of Bishop (California).
Rock type: granite.
Difficulty level: from easy to extreme.
Season: from autumn to spring.
Further details: in a desert region, but close to the Sierra Nevada; winter climbing is in the warm with snowy peaks in the background.

YOSEMITE
How to get there: situated in California, two hours north of Fresno, along highway 41.
Rock type: granite.
Difficulty level: from easy to extreme.
Season: spring and autumn.
Further details: besides the famous Camp Four blocks, there are other bouldering areas discovered more recently.

ROCKLANDS
How to get there: situated in the Cederberg Natural Reserve, three hours north of Cape Town, near the town of Clanwilliam.
Rock type: quartz granite.
Difficulty level: from easy to extreme.
Season: spring and autumn.
Further details: this is an immense and wild place. There are about a hundred boulders that have already been done, and thousands still unclimbed. Be particularly careful of snakes; many are deadly.

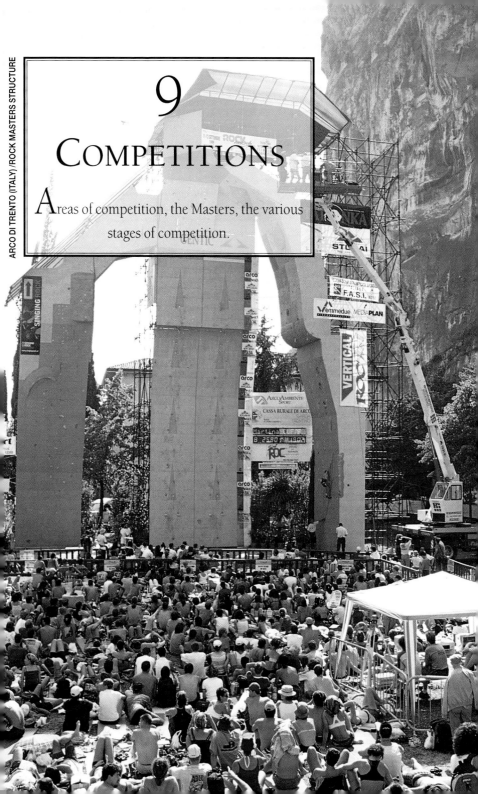

9
COMPETITIONS

Areas of competition, the Masters, the various stages of competition.

INTRODUCTION

All official competitions have been taking place on artificial walls for several years now, for three fundamental reasons:
– to ensure that all the competitors climb in identical conditions (the grip on rock is much more likely to vary with changes in weather conditions);
– to organize competitions in places that are easily accessible to the public;
– to avoid spoiling natural rock walls by continually setting out new routes for competitors.

Routes with resin hand and footholds are set out on these artificial structures; they recall the lines and movements of routes on rock, but they are usually much more physically demanding and have compulsory sections.

AREAS OF COMPETITION

Three specialized areas of competition can be distinguished:
• Difficulty
• Bouldering
• Speed

Difficulty trials take place on high walls, on routes fitted out in accordance with the rules of cliff climbing, and were the first to be officially recognized (the first round of the World Cup difficulty trials took place in 1989). The other official fixtures at an international level are biennial events: the World Championship in "on-sight" attempts, and the European Championship, which alternates with the World Cup.

Below: the structure at Vaux-en-Velin (France), where the first international indoor competition was hosted.

There are also national difficulty trials in most countries where climbing is practiced.

Above: 1999 bouldering World Cup at Bardonecchia (Italy).

Bouldering trials involve short intense sequences on low walls, with thick mattresses at the base to safeguard climbers from inevitable falls. In some European and American locations, from the start of the nineties, unofficial competitions in bouldering were organized, which over time involved ever greater numbers of competitors and spectators. In 1999 bouldering was given official recognition and included as a distinct area of climbing in its own right, with a World Cup circuit.

Speed trials take place on walls similar to those used for difficulty trials, but with a top rope, and on easy routes. Speed competitions usually operate on instant elimination, and obviously the person who completes the course in the quickest time wins. Speed competitions are spectacular to watch, but as far as technique and real sporting merit are concerned, they have much less value than the other two areas of competition. This is because completing a competition route in record time demands excellent co-ordination, agility, and quick reactions, but does not demand a particularly high level overall. Speed trials also have a World Cup circuit and a World Championship in "on-sight" attempts which is usually combined with the difficulty World Championship.

Over the next few pages the features of difficulty and bouldering will be analyzed in more depth.

Difficulty

This is today seen as the most prestigious area of competition, both because it is the longest running, and because it is in fact the most complex and requires longer and more intense training. On a physical level competitors must work on all aspects of training: power, stamina, continuity, technique, and tactics; in other words they must have excellent all-round fitness.

In difficulty competitions, competitors need to perform at an extremely high level for a relatively long time. But top performance also involves competitive tactics and the technique that uses least energy. It is not just the strongest, but the one who is also the most skilful who wins.

How a difficulty competition operates

In the days before the competition, routes of increasing difficulty for the different stages of the competition (open, quarter-finals, semi-finals, and finals) are plotted by officially recognized course plotters.

Competitors tackle the courses "on sight," which means that they can neither try out nor see the routes prior to the competition. Near to the competition structure is a warm-up zone where the competitors are kept in isolation, remaining there until they are called out for a collective viewing of the course, during which they look carefully at the line they will have to take, and attempt to grasp and memorize the movements that will be necessary. After being allowed a few minutes to visualize the route, the competitors are taken back into isolation again and then called out one by one to make their attempt.

Routes are climbed with a bottom rope, and certain safety criteria must be respected during the climb: according to

Below: in difficulty trials the winner is the one who reaches the highest point on the structure; left, the 1999 competition in Lipsia (Germany).

152

Above: in difficulty trials there is a time limit for each attempt, but how quickly you climb is not relevant.

the rules it is in fact not allowed to skip the use of any karabiner (the quick-draws are already in position), and competitors are always stopped if they go beyond the last possible hold from which the rope can be threaded through the quick-draw. In this way dangerous falls are avoided.

The winner is the one who climbs highest; in the case of a draw, competitors take part in a rematch, and if there is a draw in the rematch as well, then there has to be a superfinal to determine the winner.

Obviously there is a time limit for completing the trial, but if two competitors climb to the same height, it is irrelevant whether one is quicker than the other.

Psychologically, difficulty trials are very stressful for the competitors, because the long hours spent in isolation really put their nerves to the test. They may remain in the warm-up zone for up to 8 to 10 hours in one day. Every time they complete an attempt they are called back into isolation, so that the course plotters can dismantle the routes that have already been completed and set up the courses for the next rounds out of sight of the competitors. So self-control is just as important as physical fitness.

Finally, during the trial competitors must be completely clearheaded. Mistakes are not permitted; all the different movements test ability to the limit, so competitors must know how to plot their moves, as well as being assured that they have the power to perform them, and find resting points that allow them to relax their muscles and partly recover their energy.

The men's finals of the World Cup have a difficulty rating of 8a+/8b, while the women's are 7c+/8a. It is rare that more than one competitor reaches the chain which means completing the course (often none does), since climbing "on sight" at these levels, with the added pressure of competition, is extremely difficult. The level of the climbers that reach the final is usually so close anyway that a competition is often won or lost by a single movement.

From the top: brothers François and Arnaud Petit (France), winners of two and one World Cups respectively, and Liv Sansoz (France), many times a world champion.
Left: Katie Brown (USA), winner of numerous international competitions.

Bouldering

As has already been said, bouldering is a new arrival on the official competition circuit. The first round of the World Cup was well attended by spectators, and attracted a large number of competitors who specialize in this area of climbing.

Very few climbers prepare for both types of competition, as the training required for the two is very different. In bouldering competitors work especially on strength and reactions, since in competition many boulders require dynamic movements and sudden jumps, and also, from a technical point of view, precision of movement.

Training is more straightforward and less demanding than that required for difficulty competitions, but while there are fewer factors involved, competitors need to be gifted with a lot of natural strength, much greater than a serious competitor could ever achieve solely by training.

How a bouldering competition operates

As with difficulty competitions, the boulders are prepared by course plotters in the days preceding the competition, and the competitors are subject to the same conditions: they warm up in an isolation zone and cannot watch the others competing. The structures, or blocks, on which the bouldering courses are set up, are 3–4m

Above: Italian Marzio Nardi taking part in an international competition in Cortina (Italy).

(10 to 13 feet) high, and have various different angles. Crash mats are positioned under each block for the inevitable falls.

On each course the final hold, or top, is clearly indicated, on which competitors must clasp both hands for a few seconds before successful completion of the boulder can be claimed. Then there is the "bonus hold" (halfway stage), after an initial selective sequence, which is worth a certain amount. Below the bonus hold no points are allocated. This is obviously because the act of bouldering is so short that what really matters is whether or not the boulder is successfully completed.

Contestants have six minutes to solve each challenge (there are between four and eight for each phase of the competition), and six minutes to recover between challenges. Unlike the difficulty competitions, the competitor may make several attempts within the time. The blocks are laid out in such a way that during the recovery minutes it is not possible to watch the other contestants attempting the next challenges.

The winner is the one who successfully completes the most boulders in the least attempts. In working out who has won, the following factors are taken into account:

• Reaching the top – number of attempts made, and, in the event of the boulder not being completed,

• Bonus hold – number of attempts made.

These competitions are grueling for all the competitors on a physical level, but less taxing mentally, because there is always a second or third chance at each challenge, whereas there is no second chance in difficulty competitions.

Below: Cristian Brenna in the World Cup at Bardonecchia (Italy) in 1999.
Top: Riccardo Scarian (Italy) falls during an attempt at Cortina.

THE MASTERS

The masters are competitions that are not part of the official circuit, and may be by invitation or open. Some of them have become especially prestigious fixtures, events that are not to be missed by the spectators and highly coveted by competitors, because they represent certain important milestones in the history of competitive sport climbing.

Foremost among them all is the Rock Master at Trento (Italy). Organized for the first time in 1986, it had huge influence, together with Sportroccia at Bardonecchia (Italy), on the development of competitions in other parts of Europe and in the rest of the world, and it has remained the key event for all fans of this sport.

When the World Cup circuit first came into existence (1989), the organizers at Arco preferred not to be included, and the Rock Master, which takes place every year in the second weekend in September, became the most prestigious competition by invitation, in which the protagonists of the worldwide climbing scene compete against each other.

Another highlight for competitors and fans is the Master of Serre Chevalier (France), first contended in 1990, which has become just as prestigious as that of Arco, with one major difference: it is a Masters competition (in that it does not form part of the World Cup circuit and does not compete for that title) but it is open, which means that anyone can compete in the eliminatory phase of the competition. The best 14 male and 10 female competitors according to international rankings are automatically invited to participate in the semifinals. Others can win themselves a place by getting to the top few positions of the open round, an extremely arduous undertaking.

At both of these events the competition follows a rather particular pattern. Whereas in normal competitions all attempts are made on sight, both at Arco and at Serre Chevalier one of the two trials is a worked route, of extreme difficulty, which the contestants have half an hour to try out, in a preparatory phase before the competition itself. Then there is another major difference

Below: Belgian Muriel Sarkany, winner of Rock Master 1999, on the structure at Serre Chevalier (France).

between the two Masters: at Arco all competitors take part in both the on-sight route (the first day) and the redpoint route (second day). Their final position is given by the total number of meters climbed in both attempts. At Serre Chevalier, however, the competitors who have been invited compete in the semifinal beside those who have won the open, on an on-sight route. Only the best from this stage go through to the final (as in the World Cup competitions), and thus have the chance of attempting the redpoint route, on which they will then compete to decide the winner.

Besides these two competitive milestones, where the specialty is obviously difficulty, other Masters competitions in difficulty and bouldering are becoming set

fixtures for many competitors, and every year these prove to be a powerful draw for spectators (there also large prizes for the contestants). One such event is the summer Extreme Games, which take place in June in the United States, in a different location every year. This event is organized by the American sports television channel, ESPN, and all the best athletes of sports that are defined as extreme, and are at the same time spectacular (including sport climbing), take part. A competition is organized for each sport, with very attractive prize money to be won. After a number of years in which difficulty and speed contests featured, in 1999 the XGAMES switched to bouldering in order to try out a new competition formula, abandoning difficulty trials, but keeping speed trials as a spectacular event.

Left: the 1998 Xgames in San Diego (USA).
Top: Cristian Brenna, winner at Serre Chevalier (France) in 1999, on the night of the finals.

KEY EVENTS

July 1985
The first international rock climbing competition, SportRoccia 85, takes place in Bardonecchia (Italy). The winners are German Stefan Glowacz and Frenchwoman Catherine Destivelle.

Patrick Edlinger.

SportRoccia 85.

March 1986
First international competition in France, at Vaulx-en-Velin, on an artificial wall. The winners are Jackie Godoffe and Isabelle Patissier, both French.

July 1986
In Arco di Trento and Bardonecchia (Italy) the competition is divided into two trials. The overall winners are Patrick Edlinger and Catherine Destivelle, both French.

September 1987
Arco di Trento becomes a Rock Master, a trial by invitation, with one on sight and one redpoint route, a notable departure from the norm. Winners are Stefan Glowacz and American Lynn Hill.

Isabelle Patissier.

The first Rock Master in action.

June 1988

In Snowbird (USA) the best climbers in the world compete on courses set out on the wall of a building. Patrick Edlinger and Catherine Destivelle are the winners. This is the first major competition to be organized in the United States.

Catherine Destivelle.

September 1988

At Arco di Trento (Italy) the Rock Master

Stefan Glowacz

takes place on an artificial structure. The winners are Stefan Glowacz and Patrick Edlinger, and Lynn Hill.

May 1989

The UIAA World Cup is inaugurated in Leeds (England). It is the first international competition to take place in England, which has opposed competitions until now. The winners are Englishman Jerry Moffat and American Robyn Erbersfield.

Jerry Moffat and Ben Moon.

November 1989

Following Leeds (England), La Riba (Spain), Bardonecchia (Italy), Snowbird

Luisa Jovane at Yalta.

(USA), Vrasta (Bulgaria), Yalta (Russia), and Lyon (France), the first Sport Climbing World Cup comes to an end. Englishman Simon Nadin and Frenchwoman Nanette Raybaud are the winners.

July 1990

The first Master at Serre Chevalier (France) is held. For the first time there is a Russian standing at the top of the podium, Salavat Rakmetov.

Salavat Rakmetov.

The women's champion is Isabelle Patissier.

October 1991

The first Difficulty World Championship is held in Frankfurt (Germany). Frenchman François Legrand and Susi Good from Switzerland are the champions.

François Legrand.

In the same month, the World Cup taking place in Tokyo marks the first occasion that an international competition takes place in an Asian country.

Yuji Hirayama.

September 1992

The first European Championship takes place in Frankfurt (Germany), on the same structure as in the previous year. The victors are also the same as in the World Championship.

Lynn Hill.

June 1995
Sport climbing makes its first appearance at the XGAMES, an American extreme sports event. These first games are won by Englishman Ian Vickers and American Robyn Erbersfield.

1997
The Top Rock Challenge begins, a European circuit of bouldering competitions, which is instantly successful in attracting participants.

Top Rock Challenge.

1999
The first official circuit of the bouldering World Cup takes place. The winners are Italian Christian Core and Frenchwoman Stephanie Bodet.

Robyn Erbersfield.

Christian Core.

10

ARTIFICIAL
CLIFFS

Artificial indoor structures. Developments
to date and outlook for the future.

How they evolved

Around the beginning of the eighties, the first artificial walls began to appear in some European tourist resorts and sports centers. They were made of reinforced cement, with an outline that was vaguely reminiscent of mountains, and with hand and footholds screwed into resin. It was a great novelty, which offered everyone the chance to try climbing in complete safety. Then, in some French and American cities, the walls of certain buildings were fitted out for climbing, a bold and original idea.

At Snowbird (USA), in 1989, the World Cup competition took place on the façade of a hotel.

Top: the traditional artificial structure of a difficulty competition.
Facing page: climbing gyms can now be found all over the place.

As well as training on boulders, the climbers of a few decades ago began to construct homemade practice blocks, with wooden holds and ledges for traction and suspension. In the basements of some houses the first sloping panels of the bouldering type could be found, on which it was possible to recreate without ropes the movements and effort of cliff climbing.

The way in which artificial walls and training structures became more widespread and subsequently developed went hand in hand with developments in the competitive world. After the first few years of competitions on rock, this had been definitively converted to using artificial walls.

From the end of the eighties onwards almost all competition structures were constructed with resin or treated wood panels, and so these too began to make their appearance in gyms in cities around the world. The general tendency, when recreational structures are being built, is to make them fairly high, for climbing with ropes, so that they can be used for both teaching and training.

In the nineties, again thanks to developments in the competitive world and in training methods, low walls, with mattresses below them, also began to spring up, such as top climbers had long since built in their own houses.

Low walls

These walls, with various different slants and made of fibreglass reinforced plastic, are the most effective aid that could have been invented for specific training in sport climbing. Fixed very close together on these panels are hundreds of resin hand and footholds, of every possible shape and size, on which it is possible to pick out routes and bouldering maneuvers of every level of difficulty for working on all the different skills and techniques.

They can also be made at home; all you need is an available room and a bit of inventiveness and determination. The steeper the overhang the better they are for improving muscular strength and technique. A good wall is in fact intended for training, not necessarily for climbing. The more sloping the wall, the greater the fun, because compared to vertical walls of the same height they provide a much bigger surface that can be used.

Obviously they are also more tiring, but vertical walls, no matter how high, usually become boring after about ten minutes; it is one thing to climb on a cliff on a lovely challenging slab, it is quite another to train on monotonous vertical indoor structures.

The ideal, if you are able to build a wall, is to build it with different angles, so as to introduce more variety into your training.

The indoor structures room

In the last few years there has been a massive boom in artificial indoor structures. Many gyms house high walls for climbing courses and bouldering walls for training. Thanks to these structures being so widely available, everyone can now try out climbing, which is also often suggested as an excellent way of keeping fit, in that it is very much an all-round exercise, which tones and builds up all the muscles of the body in a balanced way.

Left: overhanging walls are ideal for training purposes.

practising it in a natural environment. They may well hold their courses in city gyms, but their aim should be to succeed in communicating to beginners the desire to move on from resin to rock.

So you may well take up climbing as a valid alternative to other activities that are more repetitive and less stimulating, which are also usually practiced in the gym, and then find that it turns into a real passion.

It can certainly be said that artificial structures, by bringing climbing within the reach of most people, have had a very positive effect on the development of this sport. It is then up to the instructors to get people to understand the spirit of climbing and the beauty of

With artificial walls it is possible to recreate in a gym all the types of situations that may be encountered in the wild.

Rock or plastic?

Competition routes, built on artificial structures, often force the climber into breathtaking and extremely difficult maneuvers, quite unlike natural routes, which for their part can almost always be interpreted in different ways that are not available on plastic.

These two types of climbing appear similar, but in reality have many differences. In fact, anyone competing at a certain level has to do very specific training on artificial structures. There are great rock climbers who have never had much success in competition, and vice versa, successful competitors who cannot reproduce on cliffs the levels of climbing that they achieve on plastic. There are also climbers who first started on resin, in inner city gyms, who sometimes even end up winning major competitions, but unfortunately have not grasped the beauty of climbing in the midst of nature: the pleasure of being in contact with the rock; the desire to travel the world in search of new cliffs; the satisfaction of

being able to recognize different types of limestone and granite; and the excitement of climbing on a type of rock that has never been attempted before.

It is mostly climbers of recent generations who have missed out on this whole culture; for many of them what counts is not so much the beauty of the location, but their own performance.

Fortunately the number of cliff enthusiasts continues to increase, despite the growing popularity of artificial walls.

Rock has not gone out of fashion, and great climbers, who live on in memory and inspire dreams, are in fact those who win competitions, and also complete, open, and free routes in locations all over the world, where extremely difficult levels of climbing are combined with the spectacular surroundings of rocks and nature.

Indoor training should always be undertaken with the aim of becoming a better climber on rock.

11
TRAINING

Apparatus and how to get started.
Training programmes and methodology.

TRAINING APPARATUS

Rock

The most essential apparatus, rock, should be the starting point and the end point for anyone who loves this sport. It is on rock that you really learn how to climb, that both technical and psychological aspects come into play, and that you finally get the rewards for all your training.

and stimulate isolated groups of muscles, creating sequences of movements that are tailor-made for you, which would be impossible on a natural rock face.

The fingerboard

The fingerboard is a resin or wooden structure, which can be bought, or made with a bit of patience, on which there are notches of different shapes and sizes. The advantage of it is that you can set it up at home, even if you

Walls

Artificial walls, obligatory training apparatus for anyone who does sport climbing at competition level, provide excellent practice for everyone. On the wall you can work specifically on the skills that you lack

have very little space, as it fits neatly above a door. It is an extremely useful piece of apparatus for working specifically on developing strength in your arms and forearms and strength and resistance in your fingers.

The bar

The bar, found in any gym, which can also be set up at home, is particularly useful for those starting training, because it offers an excellent hold for pull-ups and dead-hangs. It is also useful for working on abdominal muscles in a hanging position, an exercise that more than any other replicates the effort used in climbing.

Weights

Working with weights is very useful when you want to work on your overall strength and as a complement for more specific types of training. It is a good idea to do a two or three month cycle of weight training every year, to have a good foundation for working on more specific training.

GENERAL FITNESS

Before starting work on your muscles and on more specific aspects you need to build up a solid foundation so as to be generally well-toned all over and to improve your cardiovascular fitness.

Jogging and cycling are excellent for this purpose, though they are aerobic exercises that should always be treated as complementary activities, as climbing is predominantly an anaerobic sport.

Running

It is recommended that you do this twice a week, starting with 20 minutes, if you are not used to it, and working gradually up to a maximum of 60 minutes. You should always run slowly, or jog, which means keeping your pulse rate between 120 and 140, the optimum level for getting air to your muscles and burning off fat. However, running tends, if overdone, to make the leg muscles shorter and thicker, and to diminish the elasticity of tendons and ligaments, so it is important not to do more than easy jogging, and to spend at least 20 minutes stretching after each run.

Cycling

Whether on a road bike or a mountain bike, this is an excellent alternative to running. You should do one or two fairly long outings a week, of between 90 and 120 minutes, to activate the process of burning off fat. You should cycle at a fairly sustained pace for the aerobic exercise to be effective. To avoid building up your leg muscles too much it is best always to use low gears and not to cycle in too hilly an area. Again, after a cycling session it is important to spend 20–30 minutes stretching.

PHYSICAL TRAINING

Let us now see which are the basic exercises used to build up the muscles of the torso and arms, which are needed for climbing.

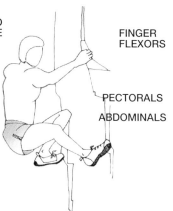

DELTOID MUSCLE

TERES MINOR AND TERES MAJOR

RHOMBOID

LATISSIMUS DORSI MUSCLE

FINGER FLEXORS

PECTORALS

ABDOMINALS

Abdominals

1 With your knees bent and your arms behind your neck, flex your torso.

2 With knees bent and arms behind your neck, flex your torso while twisting.

3 Sitting with arms on the ground behind you and knees bent, raise your pelvis.

4 Hanging from the bar or wall bars, bring knees to your chest. If you can, pause at 90° when lowering.

Pectorals

<u>Without apparatus:</u>
5 Press-ups: hands planted on the ground, slightly wide of your chest and pointing inwards.

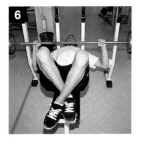

<u>With weights:</u>
6–7 Push-ups with the barbell on the flat bench.

Triceps

<u>Without apparatus:</u>
8 Press-ups: hands under your chest and pointing to your chin.
9 With your hands behind you on a chair or a bench and your legs straight out in front, raise and lower yourself on your arms.

<u>With weights:</u>
10 Stretching out your arm with a dumbbell. Your other arm helps the one performing the exercise to maintain the position.

Biceps

At the bar:

11 Pull yourself up, grasping the bar with palms of your hands turned away from you. If you cannot complete the pull-up you may get a friend to help you.

With weights:

12 Seated on a bench with your legs apart, grasp a dumbbell, with the elbow of the arm that is working leaning on the inside of your thigh: bend and straighten your arm completely.

Then do the same exercise with the palm of your hand facing down: this will work the finger extensors and brachioradialis muscle (forearm).

Deltoids

At the bar:

14 Alternate side lifts with the dumbbells: works on the central section of the muscle. Keep your knees slightly bent so as not to tire your back.

15 Alternate front lifts with dumbbells: works the front part of the deltoid. Make sure your back is supported.

16 Rowing movements at the bench: with the knee and arm on one side leaning on the bench, flex the other arm to bring the dumbbell to the height of your waist; works the rear part of the deltoid, and the teres minor and major.

Dorsals

At the bar:

17–18 Pull-ups with your hands wide apart and palms facing away from your face.

If you go to a gym you can do the same exercise on the "lat machine," gradually increasing the load.

Forearm and finger flexors

19 Grasp a dumbbell and roll your wrists, imagining that you are twisting a rope.

20–21 Hang from the bar or a good hand-hold with both arms and then with only one, and try to do it for a little longer each time.

Exercises with weights are always good, no matter what state your muscles are in to start with. Obviously, as you improve the weights will increase and exercises will become more specific, aimed at strength and stamina.

Similarly you will also do pull-ups and dead-hangs not just at the bar, but also on handholds and notches on the fingerboard, and with additional weight.

AGILITY

In climbing, agility makes for more efficiency: it is an important physical quality that allows you to find positions in which you use the least energy and in which you can resolve very technically demanding sections, although you do not need to be as agile as you might need to be for other sports (e.g. artistic or rhythmic gymnastics).

As regards legs, the basic movements are:
– Loosen the joints of your pelvis so as to get closer to the wall and to find the right balance to link movements together without relying entirely on strength.
– Raise your legs high, to be able to reach very high footholds.

It is also important to have generally supple joints, as this can prevent you doing yourself an injury by making some unnaturally forced movement, such as the Egyptian, or twisting your shoulders. Spend some time working on agility before and after every training session with weights, if you want to avoid the muscles becoming hypertrophied and overshortening, thus losing elasticity and risking injury every time they are used in a stretched position.

Before a workout, stretching lengthens the muscular fibers and encourages the muscle to contract in the best way possible, using its entire length and thus producing more power. After a workout it helps to eliminate any residual contraction in the muscle and lengthens the fibers again, thus preventing them from losing elasticity. It is essential to think about all your muscles and joints when you are working on agility; it may be important to stretch your legs and your pelvis, but it is equally important not to neglect your torso, arms, and hands.

Stretching your fingers and keeping the tendons elastic is particularly important in reducing the risk of injury, as inflammation of the finger tendons and stretched or torn sheaths are the main climbing ailments.

So take careful note of the following stretches and agility exercises, which should always be done before and after a training session or climbing:

Abdominal muscles

1 Stretched out on the ground, with your legs completely straight and your pelvis in contact with the floor, raise yourself on your arms, arching your back. Arch back as far as you can, making sure that you do not raise your pelvis .

Side muscles

2 On your knees, stretch one leg out to the side while supporting yourself on the opposite arm. Your free arm should be stretched over your head, completing the arch formed by your body.

Hamstring (rear thigh)

3 Lean forward from the waist and touch the floor with your palms, if possible. Also good for the calf muscles.

4 Sit on the floor with one leg straight and the other bent, so your foot is against the opposite thigh. Grasp your ankle and try to bring your chest down to your knee. This is also good for the muscles at the side of your back.

Front of thigh muscles (quadriceps)

5 Sit on the floor with both legs bent, one behind you and the other with its foot resting against the opposite thigh. Supporting yourself on your arms, lean back without raising your knees or buttocks.

6 A variation of 5. If you can, lean your torso further back until your shoulders touch the ground.

Inner thigh muscles

7 Lie on the floor with your legs wide apart, straight, and leaning against a wall; allow the weight of your legs to stretch the muscles.

Inner thigh muscles and hip joint flexibility

8 Sit with your legs wide open and bend both legs so that you bring both feet together at your crotch. Grasp your toes with your hands and lean forwards, keeping your back straight.

9 Lying on your back, bend both legs with the soles of your feet touching, and bring them up to your crotch. Allow your legs to sink to the floor.

10 Take up a squatting position, with your feet well apart and pointing to the side, and your knees as wide open as possible. Keeping your back straight, push your thighs outwards with your elbows.

Lower back muscles (lumbar region)

11 Squat down until you are sitting on your heels, with your feet flat on the ground, and your arms stretched out between your knees.

12 With your hands on the nape of your neck, push your head forwards and down.

Back of neck muscle
13 Lying on the ground, bring your legs over your head and try to place your knees on the ground on either side of your head. This is also good for your shoulders.

Muscles at sides of back
14 Holding on to a piece of apparatus, bend your torso over and arch your back.

Latissimus dorsi and arm muscles
15 Find a solid handhold, and hang onto it with your arm stretched right out. Push your body backwards, with your legs slightly bent, to find the position in which your back is stretched.

Latissimus dorsi and triceps
16 Standing with feet wide apart, your arms above your head, pull one arm down towards the nape of your neck, and bend your torso sideways at the same time.

Triceps
17 In a kneeling position, grasp one elbow, keeping your back very straight, and force that arm towards the middle of your back.

Pectoral and front deltoid muscles
18 Stand with your back to the wall bars and hold onto them at shoulder height. Lean your body forwards.
19 Stand with your back to the wall bars, reach one arm out behind and place it against the beam, then force your shoulders forward with a rotational movement of the chest.

Rear deltoid muscle
20 Kneeling and with your torso straight, grasp the back of your elbow with your arm bent at shoulder height. Push your elbow towards the opposite shoulder.

Shoulder flexibility
21 Standing in front of a piece of furniture or wall bars, reach your arms out behind you with your hands together and grasp the bars with your thumbs laid flat. Walk your feet out from the base of the bars and squat down, keeping your arms above you.

22 Seated with your legs apart, lean back on your arms, placing them as far from your body as you can, with your palms flat. Slide your body forwards to increase the stretch.

Biceps

23 Kneeling down, lower your head to the ground, with your face turned to the arm that is bent with its elbow high. Stretch the other arm out to the side and lower your shoulder to the ground.

Muscles of the forearm

24 Kneel down on all fours with your back very straight, and your fingers pointing towards your knees. Rock your body backwards to obtain the maximum stretch.

25 Stand in front of a wall and stretch your arms forwards with your hands laid flat on the wall, fingers pointing down. To get the best stretch possible, bend your legs slightly.

Finger flexor muscles

26 With your arms stretched out in front of your body, pull your fingers backwards onto your wrist. This is also good for the palm.

27 The arm that you are working on should be stretched out in front of you with the palm upwards. Pull each finger down individually. More effective for the finger flexors.

To obtain the best possible muscle lengthening and joint flexibility it is a good idea to do some stretching every day, and also to remember the following:

• Each position should be held for at least 30 seconds for the exercise to be effective.

• Your movements should be slow and gradual.

• Stretching should be almost a static exercise, without any jerks.

• If you feel pain it is a sign that you should stop.

• While doing each stretch you should breathe deeply, exhaling during the phase when the muscle is most stretched.

TRAINING

Climbing itself is the best form of training; by increasing the intensity of your efforts, in other words by attempting more difficult routes, you will make progress. This may seem a trite thing to say, but it is worthwhile bearing in mind. Climbers who want to progress from level 6a to 6b should be aware that practicing on 5+ routes too often will make them regress.

Many climbers claim that they do no training whatsoever, whereas they spend three or four days a week climbing, either on cliffs or artificial structures. These people are training without realizing it, but without a method they do not always succeed in turning their efforts into improved performance. Climbing as the sole form of training is not sufficient; even if you use every muscle in your body you will not necessarily progress beyond a certain level. Successful training depends on several factors:

• Set yourself a realistic target; when you reach it you can set another;
• Find out by means of tests what your shortcomings are;
• Develop your abilities in a scientific way;
• Vary the type, intensity, and number of the exercises as much as possible;
• Do not overdo your training; you need strength to climb, but strength alone does not make a good climber.

Training is based on three different types of exercises:

General exercises
These have already been discussed and include those, which improve the oxygenation of muscles, work on particular muscle groups, and improve flexibility, but do not replicate the movements of climbing.

Specific exercises
These involve muscle groups essential for climbers, and put them to work in a climbing context or similar.

Climbing
Climbing is not only for putting your improved physique to the test, but also the time when you refine your movements and technique, essential for making the most of your efforts.

TRAINING METHODOLOGY IN CLIMBING

Objective performance

To see a real improvement in your performance you need above all to know the three components that contribute to it:
• Conditioned energy source
• Cognitive method
• Emotions

Conditioned energy resources: strength, resistance, and continuity

Unlike many sports, the effort involved in sport climbing is of a very complex nature. It is a combination of several energy channels, and during the course of a climb the interaction of strength, resistance, and continuity is necessary; these are the main sources of conditioned energy always called upon. Climbers who want to be thoroughly and effectively prepared should therefore take these complementary aspects into account in their training.

During a training session, if these energy sources are to be improved, you should always be working close to your limit. These energy sources show themselves in the number of movements you make: when counting them you take only hand movements into account, and not foot movements, because it is in your arms, obviously, that tiredness is felt.

Strength

This comes into play at between 1 and 10 maximum energy movements. It can be further divided into two parts:
• pure strength, which is developed in the first five maximum energy movements and not after, and calls mostly upon the activation of nerve fibers (anaerobic exercise not producing lactic acid).
• resistance, which develops between the fifth and the tenth movement, and mobilizes the basic energy reserve (anaerobic exercise producing lactic acid)

Examples of strength training

Exercises at the fingerboard, with extra

weight. First calculate your maximum weight (= body weight + lifted weight).

– Sinusoidal method of pull-ups at the fingerboard or bar (3 pull-ups at 90% – 2 pull-ups at 95% of your maximum weight, repeated 3 times, or 2 at 95% and 1 at 98%, repeated 3 times, for pure strength, with 1 minute recovery between exercises, and 3 minutes' recovery between each set)

– Pyramidal pull-ups at the fingerboard or bar (2–3–5–8, with 1 minute recovery. Percentages: 95%, 90%, 85%, 75%)

– Maximum weight dead-hangs on the fingerboard (max. 5 seconds)

– Bouldering on a wall, with generous recovery time (approx. 3 minutes)

– Exercise with weights: 3 sets of a maximum of 4–6 repetitions, with 3 minutes' recovery between the sets.

Examples of tests for evaluating strength

Arms maximum strength

Hang from the bar with a weight attached to your harness and try to pull yourself up. If you can do this easily, increase the weight, resting completely (five minutes) between attempts, until you can only just complete a pull-up with great difficulty. The maximum weight is the sum of your own weight and the extra weight. The arms and fingers maximum strength is the same, but on the 2 cm notch.

Fingers maximum strength

Hang from a 3 cm notch, with a weight attached to your harness.

Resistance

This comes into play when you manage to combine from 10 to 30–40 movements.

It is the ability to work at 70% of your own maximum strength for a fairly short period of time (1–4 minutes). As with strength, resistance can also be divided into short resistance (from 10 to 20 movements), in which the muscular fibers are still working without oxygen, and long resistance (from 20 to 40 movements), in

which an aerobic component begins to play a part.

Examples of resistance training
– A set of 3 circuits of 20 movements – 5 minutes' rest between circuits (short resistance)
– A set of 3 circuits of 30–40 movements – 5 minutes' rest between circuits (long resistance)
– Recovery time between sets (approx. 15 minutes)
– Resistance on the fingerboard: 3 sets of 10–minute workouts. Do a dead-hang or a pull-up every minute, resting only for the seconds remaining in that same minute. e.g. 20 seconds' dead-hang on the 2 cm notch, 40 seconds' recovery. 3–5 minutes' recovery between each workout.
– Exercises with weights: 3 sets of 8–10 repetitions, with 1–1.5 minutes' recovery. Specific resistance tests are not important: all you need is to find circuits on the wall that you have difficulty in completing, which means always working close to your limit.

Continuity
Continuity is not a precise energy source and it is typical of the complexity of the effort required in climbing. It may be said that continuity corresponds to your capacity for active recovery between two or more sessions of force and resistance.

It is a workout of more than 40 movements and differs from resistance in that it involves prolonged effort at a level of intensity determined by the necessity of resting during a route. Sections of a route between rest points are quite long and intense enough to tire out your muscles and it would probably be impossible to complete them without rests.

Examples of continuity training
– Try to complete tough circuits of 50/60 movements, with a partial rest half way – rest for between 5 to 10 minutes between each circuit.
– Choose a circuit of 60–75 movements which stretches you to your limit, divide it into 3 sections of 20–25 movements, and rest between sections for the same amount of time that you have been climbing (max. 2 minutes), and then rest completely (15 minutes).
– Try to complete a circuit of 30–40 movements, making 6 movements forwards, and 3 backwards.

THE COGNITIVE ASPECT
Technique and tactics

Working on your conditioned energy sources is not enough, on its own, to guarantee excellent results, since there are, as all top level athletes and climbers know, two other aspects that must be taken into consideration if you are to improve your performance: technique and tactics. These are two qualities that allow you to conserve energy during your efforts.

A good technique ensures that you make best use of your movement patterns and can thus choose the best position to get through each section.

Tactics are the ability to "read" the route as well as possible, and so to find good rest points, understand which are the best holds to use when clipping quick-draws, and also what sort of rhythm (how fast to progress) it is best to use during the climb. These two qualities are improved if you do a lot of "on sight" climbing, where you get used to quickly solving a succession of new problems. The same is true on known routes, when you try to find the optimum movements, new resting points, and thus store away ideas that can also be made good use of in your climbing.

Making a training programme

In order to make an intelligent training program you must first have a clear idea of your objectives.

Climbers who are preparing for a season of competition follow a fairly lengthy program, which may extend over a period of six months, divided into three cycles of two months each. They work in turn on strength, resistance, and continuity, with booster strength sessions during resistance and continuity training, so that they always keep their muscles highly stimulated and thus work out at a high intensity level. If, however, your aim is to improve your own performance on the cliff, while continuing to climb at quite a high level and to enjoy yourself even during training periods, then it is pointless making yourself a training cycle with workouts that are too specific or too heavy. You are better off following a constant, all-round type of workout, which develops all your skills all the time.

It is vital that you always remember to vary the exercises that you do, even if you are fairly constantly in training: switch exercises at the fingerboard, try out new circuits each month, and try to go climbing in different locations.

EXAMPLE OF A MONTHLY TRAINING PROGRAMME

Three days' training and two days' cliff climbing

1st week:
1st day – strength;
2nd day – strength;
3rd day – resistance

2nd week:
1st day – strength;
2nd day – resistance;
3rd day – continuity

3rd week:
1st day – resistance;
2nd day – continuity;
3rd day – continuity

4th week–winding down (working at 50% of the 2nd week):
1st day – strength;
2nd day – resistance;
3rd day – continuity

– You should always be well rested for working on strength.
– It is important to vary the exercises so as to always provide new stimulus for your body.
– Warm up properly before each workout to avoid injury.
– If you wish to improve quality x compared to y and z, draw up a training plan, focussing on x, but you must not forget to do booster sessions for y and z at least once a week.

THE EMOTIONAL ASPECT

The mind exerts an influence, that is often underestimated, on all our perceptions, thoughts, and states. In an indirect but vital way, it guides all our movements, and plays a decisive role in determining all our actions. It can exert either a positive or a negative influence on our abilities, and it is thus an important component affecting the level at which we perform.

Fear

Fear is a factor that very much hinders climbing. It arises from a feeling of insecurity, from a lack of faith in the belayer or the spotter, or in the protection that the route offers.

Obviously a little fear is equivalent to caution. However in reality, fear is almost always a totally irrational feeling, given the total absence in sport climbing of any objective danger that you need to be able to evaluate and avoid if necessary (for example, a route with old and precarious bolts). Falling may give rise to fear, even though, if you are rational about it, you know that nothing serious can happen. Cliff routes are equipped in such a way as to allow you to fall every time you do a section wrong without any negative consequences. People who climb only as second are losing sight of essential points of the mental and tactical aspect of climbing. They end up with such a total lack of stored experiences that the very thought of having to climb as leader conjures up a fear of the unknown. This mental block can only be removed by getting used to climbing in situations where a fall is very likely, always, of course, in safe conditions.

Coping with exhaustion

Even when you are enjoying climbing, exhaustion can sometimes build up progressively, bringing with it very unpleasant sensations.

Training also means learning how to cope with exhaustion and with the feelings of pain that your muscles send you when they are working in acidosis, when your forearm hardens and you need to access your last energy reserves. But you must not be a Stakhanovite; a continuous state of exhaustion must be taken seriously, and certain types of pain, for example pain in the joints, are an alarm signal that you are overloading your body or doing the wrong sort of exercise. If this happens, you need to review your training program, and reduce the weights or the number of weekly sessions.

Obviously, when you are climbing at a level close to your limit, the feeling of exhaustion is inevitable, but you must learn how to keep a clear mind at all times when climbing, compensating for the lower performance of your arm muscles by greater use of other muscle groups, such as those of the shoulders or back.

Ambition

This is the foundation of all sporting performance, but it can also work as a sort of mental block. Fear of giving up or excessive pressure from your expectations can sometimes turn an attempt on a route into a psychological trial. You need to have well balanced self-awareness, and realize that a failure on that particular route does not mean that you have been defeated.

Performance should be a source of personal satisfaction, but it should not become an obsession.

Willpower

You make progress because, basically, you want to do so. If motivation is lacking, you are likely to train in the wrong way and in a

sporadic manner, without deriving any real benefits. You must learn how to work on your own motivation, without lying to yourself: it is not enough just to say that you want to get to level 7a, you must also want to develop the means to do so. Motivation activates willpower and hence the ability to perform. How strong it is, is influenced by many factors, such as stress at work or in your home life, tiredness, and a lack of stimulating climbing partners. When you are under a lot of pressure or generally in a weakened state, it is better for you to take a break from training, and spend some time on other activities.

Just as some situations can cause a drop in motivation, others can, fortunately, stimulate it. These are subjective and totally impossible to list. It may be that a particular route has great significance for you, or you have an ambition to be better than someone else, or the stimulus of training with better climbers than yourself. It is important to be able to absorb positive situations and feelings, to create a store of mental resources to draw on when you are having difficulty in summoning up motivation. The Americans sum it all up in the well-known phrase: "It's all in your mind." Unfortunately it is not always possible to achieve all that you want, but enthusiasm and the willpower to succeed are certainly key ingredients in success. The strength of your motivation is an indication, according to recent research, of the releasable potential of physical and mental energy.

The results of some medical studies on sport show that, when motivation is very strong, the body produces substances (endorphins) that can even prevent you from feeling pain. So with sufficiently high

motivation it is possible to go beyond certain pain thresholds, releasing energy that would not normally be used.

According to the German doctor Hettinger (see table on the next page) each individual has the ability to perform at a level that does not normally reach 50% of his potential. The range of "automatic performance" (up to 15%) and that of "psychological readiness for performance" (from 15 to 35%) demand only low or medium willpower. The "mobilization of habitual energy reserves" (from 35 to 60%) demands much greater willpower.

The "independently protected reserves" (from 65 to 100%) can usually be accessed by excitement, hypnosis, or drugs (doping). Hettinger describes the zone between the range of habitual readiness and that of the independently protected reserves as the "mobilization threshold." Depending on the degree of motivation and with adequate training, this threshold can be consciously shifted, bringing it very close to the absolute performance capacity.

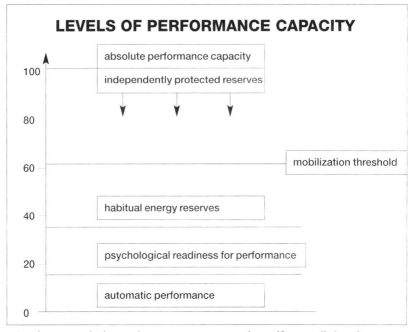

LEVELS OF PERFORMANCE CAPACITY

absolute performance capacity

independently protected reserves

mobilization threshold

habitual energy reserves

psychological readiness for performance

automatic performance

Taken from *Sport climbing, technique – tactics – training* by Wolfgang Gullich and Andreas Kubin.

It's the enjoyment that matters

Climbing is fun, and going climbing should also be a sort of escape valve, a way of regenerating yourself mentally and physically. It would be foolish to carry on climbing if it were not enjoyable ... and yet some people have such a strong desire to complete routes (at whatever the level), that they take every small failure in a very negative way, and give the impression that they are not enjoying themselves at all.

Similarly, training should not become a burden, something that you are forcing yourself to do. Therefore, if you decide to train, you should first of all think of what you like doing; an exercise tackled in the right frame of mind is most certainly more effective than one done grudgingly, because your mind and body will be in harmony. If it turns out that you really do not like training at all, then you should stick to climbing on cliffs or on boulders in your free time, but do not complain if you do not succeed in getting beyond a certain level!

© 2001 Colophon srl
San Polo 1978, 30125 Venice, Italy

Concept: Andrea Grandese
Project Management: Paolo Lazzarin
Design and Layout: Graphotek/Bruno Quattro
Text: Federica Balteri (instructor for the Italian Federation of Sport Climbing)
Consultant for the Italian Edition: Diego Bortolamedi
Illustrations: Maria Borghi, Gabriele Frione
Photography:
Archivio Artioli, Archivio Baistrocchi, Archivio Balteri, Archivio Brenna, Archivio Ferrero,
Federica Balteri, Nicholas Hobley, Guy Maddox, Francesco Panunzio, Marco Scolaris/ A.R.I.A.
Acknowledgements:
Editorial staff of Montebianco/Edisport Editoriale
Martina Artioli, Enrico Baistrocchi, Gilberto Barantani, Cristian Brenna, Benedetta Bussolati,
Nicholas Hobley, Elena Isaia, Massimo Malpezzi, Francesco Panunzio (Panolo), Marco Scolaris
Palestra New Trefor, Camp, Five Ten

Original Title: Sport Climbing

©2001 for this English edition:
Könemann Verlagsgesellschaft mbH
Bonner Str. 126, D – 50968 Cologne

Translation from Italian: Harriet de Blanco in association with
Cambridge Publishing Management
Editing: Kay Coulson in association with Cambridge Publishing Management
Typesetting: Cambridge Publishing Management
Project Management: Steven Carruthers for Cambridge Publishing Management, UK
Project Coordination: Nadja Bremse-Koob
Production: Petra Grimm

Printing and Binding: Società Torinese, Industrie Grafiche, Editoriali S.p.A., San Mauro, Italy
Printed in Italy

ISBN 3-8290-6492-6

10 9 8 7 6 5 4 3 2 1